Praise for Gabriel Fitzmaurice

'[T]he best contemporary, traditional, popular poet in English.'

Ray Olson, *Booklist* (US)

'Fitzmaurice is a wonderful poet.'

Giles Foden, *The Guardian*

'Fitzmaurice is one of Ireland's leading poets ... a master of his art.'

Books Ireland

'Ireland, particularly the South ... finds its local bard in Gabriel Fitzmaurice ... thereby making such "singing" socially responsible in a way Wordsworth would have endorsed.'

Francis O'Hare, *HU (The Honest Ulsterman)*

'[Fitzmaurice] is poetry's answer to John B. Keane.'

Fred Johnston, *Books Ireland*

'We need poets who can probe reality like this, and Fitzmaurice is doing it in style.'

Gerard Quinn, *The Kerryman*

'He has a gift for making the quotidian interesting and investing the ordinary with extraordinary significance'.

Gearóid Mac Lochlainn, *The Celtic Pen*

'Gabriel Fitzmaurice finds truths that speak to us all'.

Moyra Donaldson, *Figments* (Belfast)

'[Fitzmaurice] has...attained a folk-song-like charm and memorability that Yeats and Frost, for example, found only in old age ... Fitzmaurice is one of the most thoroughgoing poets of place, the brother in conviction of Kentucky patriot Wendell Berry and the great Orkneyman George Mackay Brown.'

Ray Olson, *Booklist* (US)

'Not unlike those of Goldsmith and Burns, these poems are endowed with charm, wit and generosity of spirit . . . He transcends sentimentality to effect what that redoubtable school inspector Matthew Arnold would recognise as 'a criticism of life' . . . His elegies and love-poems are direct, moving evocations; his poems to and about friends and neighbours will make you wish you were among them.'

James J. McAuley, The Irish Times

'Gabriel Fitzmaurice has demonstrated time and again that Moyvane, County Kerry, his heartland, is one of the global villages of our day . . . [T]he language act follows the contours of a mind meditating on the revelatory nature of the precious yet fleeting quanta of daily life . . . There is a deceptive ease to much of Fitzmaurice's work. This volume shows a spirited voice at work that is able to preserve the grain of Irish folklore in modern verse, to translate in a clear, rhythmic idiom and to look with a wise eye at the local harmonies we make of our heroes, daily routines, moments of vision, family and village life.'

Brian Coates, Poetry Ireland Review

'[T]he poetry of Gabriel Fitzmaurice is salutary . . . This is poetry of the felt experience as D. H. Lawrence would have advocated . . . Fitzmaurice's elevation of Moyvane has resonances with Oliver Goldsmith's Auburn, and Patrick Kavanagh's Shancoduff. The eternal verities of place, character, and local colour are frozen like a Vermeer . . . Gabriel Fitzmaurice's poetry is visionary and durable, unforced and deceptively simple.'

Brendan Hamill, Fortnight

The Lonesome Road

First published in 2014 by
Liberties Press
140 Terenure Road North | Terenure | Dublin 6W
Tel: +353 (1) 405 5701
www.libertiespress.com | info@libertiespress.com

Trade enquiries to Gill & Macmillan Distribution
Hume Avenue | Park West | Dublin 12
T: +353 (1) 500 9534 | F: +353 (1) 500 9595 | E: sales@gillmacmillan.ie

Distributed in the UK by
Turnaround Publisher Services
Unit 3 | Olympia Trading Estate | Coburg Road | London N22 6TZ
T: +44 (0) 20 8829 3000 | E: orders@turnaround-uk.com

Distributed in the United States by
IPM | 22841 Quicksilver Dr | Dulles, VA 20166
T: +1 (703) 661-1586 | F: +1 (703) 661-1547 | E: ipmmail@presswarehouse.com

ISBN: 978-1-909718-36-4
2 4 6 8 10 9 7 5 3 1
A CIP record for this title is available from the British Library.

Cover design by Karen Vaughan
Internal design by Liberties Press

The publishers gratefully acknowledge
financial assistance from the Arts Council.

The Lonesome Road

Collected and New Poems
1984–2014

Gabriel Fitzmaurice

LIB
ERT
IES

For Brenda
with love

Contents

Acknowledgements

This *Collected Poems* represents all the poems of mine I wish to be collected at the present time. Time and the road have whittled away at these poems till what is left now are the versions I wish to keep.

I am indebted to the editors and publishers who first published the poems which I've taken from the following collections: *Rainsong* (Beaver Row Press, Dublin, 1984), *Road to the Horizon* (Beaver Row Press, 1987), *Dancing Through* (Beaver Row Press, 1990), *The Father's Part* (Story Line Press, Oregon, 1992), *The Village Sings* (Story Line Press, Cló Iar-Chonnachta, Conamara, Peterloo Poets, Cornwall, 1996), *A Wrenboy's Carnival* (Wolfhound Press, Dublin, Peterloo Poets 2000), *I and the Village* (Marino Books, Dublin, 2002), *The Boghole Boys* (Marino Books, Cork, 2005), *Twenty One Sonnets* (Salmon Poetry, Cliffs of Moher, 2007), *Poems of Faith and Doubt* (Salmon Poetry, 2011) and *A Middle-aged Orpheus Looks Back at His Life* (Liberties Press, Dublin, 2013).

Most of the new poems have been published in *Poetry Ireland Review*, *Quadrant* (Australia) and the *Cork Literary Review*.

from Rainsong

(1984)

Portaireacht Bhéil

Who would make music hears in himself
The tune that he must play.
He lilts the inarticulate.
He wills cacophony obey.

Portaireacht Bhéil: (Irish) mouth music, lilting, humming

Lovers

Is it the clothes
Or is it the socks?
There's a sweet smell of dirt off me.
I smell of my friends –
Must take a wash.

A lunatic laughs at Mass.
(It's really a sin,
But to be normal
Is to laugh at him.)

He laughs at us –
At our cleanliness,
At our fuss.
Better to go and hustle
Like him.

Your car was wrecked,
You buy one new –
Who hasn't a ha'penny
Well God bless you.

The river,
Convulsed like a lunatic
Stormed on a table,
Is called Annamoy.
I love it
Because it's a hopeless river.
But sun, clouds, cows
Quiver in it,
Wagtails ripple over it,
While bulls trample its stones.

The village is Newtown Sandes
Called Moyvane ('The Middle Plain')
For hate of landlords.
New people don't like it.
I want to die in it.

Like the mad
Flirting with the happy and sad
And hope and the rope
And water,
The people like islanders
Await the disaster
And live.
Dogs and simpletons
Plough the midday swirl of dust and papers.

I did a line with the city,
Made love to a town,
But always that dung-sotted river
Leafed me home.

Newtown, you bastard,
You'll break me, I know:
New women won't live here,
Our women have left here
And always I grow old.

Like a dog and its master,
Like a ship on the water,
I need you, you bitch,
Newtown.

I need you, you bitch,
Newtown.

Eel

Of all the fish in the Annamoy,
We, children, feared the eel.
We harpooned him with forks
Stolen from the table.

He was like no fish we ever knew –
Ignorant of Sargasso, we created him
Of horse-hair and manure.

You couldn't kill the eel, we knew.
Even when he was wriggling on a fork,
Dusty on dry land, he lived.

We kicked him, beat him,
And still he lived.

To shackle terror
We shoved him,
We thought forever,
In the river.

Derelicts

Whenever I picture the village fools
They drool with the hump
Of benevolence on their backs.
Living in hovels as I remember,
They had the health of the rat.

They perched on the street-corner
Like crows around the carcass
Of a lamb. Stale bread and sausages
Would feed a hungry man.
Beady with the cunning of survival,
Each pecked the other from his carrion.

Children feared them like rats in a sewer –
They stoned their cabins
And the stones lay at the door.

Like priests, they were the expected,
The necessary contrary –
We bow in gratitude for mediocre lives;
We keep the crow, the rat, from the garden.
Like priests, no one mourned when they died.

When they died, we pulled down their cabins;
Then we transported a lawn
That the mad, the hopeless might be buried –
Only the strong resisting (while strong).
We kept the grass and flowerbeds neatly
But the wilderness wouldn't be put down.

Children no longer play there
(They stone it),

Nettles stalk the wild grass,
Scutch binds the stones together . . .

Then came the rats.

Hay

for my father

1
Heavy bales are hoors.
The shed is no place
If you're not too strong.
Sweat sticks
Like hay to wool
And the rhythm of hay
Is the last native dance.

Will it ever stop,
This suicidal monotone of hay?
It goes on like a depression
In the rural brain.

Hay
(Long ago the days were longer)

Hay
(Long ago the men were stronger)

Hay
(Long ago you gave a day's labour
For a day's pay)
(It didn't rain in summer long ago)

Hay Hay Hay

2
I bought a bulk milk container,
I built another shed –
Everyone advised me that

The ass-and-cart, the tank
Were dead.

My father would surely wonder now
At the size of my great herd.

I've bulldozed uneconomic ditches
That made *Garraí Beag, Fearann, Móinéar* –
This great new field I'm fencing
Has no name.

My father
Spoke to his cows in winter
In the stall.
Connor knew his herd by name –
He fed them on the long acre
And was put in jail.

There was a priest here once
Who ranted that a man
Measured his importance
In the size of his dung-hill,
The poor clout!

Nowadays
You measure your importance
In the size of your bulk container.
Shortly they'll open
'The Club of the Bulk Container:
Farmers Not Allowed'.

The good is modern –
You can't opt out.

3

Once I made wynds
In small meadows for fear of rain.
Some of the hay was green.
A friendly dog kept jumping on my back.
We had time for a fag
And porter at the gap.

Later
We milked the cows by hand
And strained the milk with a rag –
'A white cloth', we called it.

We laughed in those days
We did
We did

We laughed . . .

Garraí Beag: (Irish) The small garden
Fearann: (Irish) A field, ploughland
Móinéar: (Irish) A meadow
The long acre: The grass margin at the side of the road

Epitaph

A colossus on the playing field,
A great man for the crack,
For years he spoke to no one
But turned his sagging back on people.
Head down, he would cycle into town.

Whispers prodded that he be seen to:
'Looked after', slyly said.
Anyone could see
That his head was out of joint.
And he couldn't even hold his lonely pint.

They found him hanging in the barn: dead.
Viciousness turned almost to understanding.
Living alone, never wed . . .
'His uncle did it years before him.
Kind for him,' they said.

The crack: fun, high jinks, conviviality
Kind for him: it was in his genes, in his nature

The Skald Crow

for John Moriarty

At first I didn't know you –
You were a stranger when you came;
I fed you in winter,
I nursed you when you were lame.

You screwed your black beak
Into my brain –
You fed yourself when you were hungry;
I croaked your song.

You are stronger than hope,
Stronger than despair,
Stronger than love,
You are stronger than hate.

Against you I have no litany
But to call you *me*,
And though you'd trick me
Into felling the tree you nest on,
I'll not cut down the tree.

In the beginning, you came to me.

Wilderness

Being
Reverberates like a gun;
Swish of sea
And vultures' cry
Are one
Dripping like a rag wrung:
I could be
Infinite possibility.

In the wilderness
Is no path;
Flotsam in the desert
And the question tossed:
What is is me,
Why am I not me?
Pinstripes
And the suicide's rope.

Am wolf
And hanging man
And cauldron's bubble.

Am lamb.

Because We Love

1
On land
Ignorant of man;
In sky
Ignorant of bird;
In river
Ignorant of fish.

Knows the living
Knows the dead
Knows the murderer
And won't tell.
Won't give
Won't kill.

Separate from life
Though living;
Separate from death
Though dying.
Not opposite
Being not one.

Like man and woman.

2
Semen spurted,
Man-sweat in the womb . . .

Because we love
We're human
And can hate.

We wonder
At the sky above us,
At that beneath our feet,
Our children, like us,
Hatched in ignorance.

We die intestate.

Stale Porter

'Love is too big for people,
They only live together in the end',
I wrote, a lovesick adolescent.

Now a paunchy thirty
With marriage willowing in porter,
Velvet, lily cream,
I wonder.

She was velvet, lily cream,
And then I loved her –
And love her yet
Through froth of hate:

We ate the prawns of love.

So once again your love you banished
Leaving you alone.
Leash your gun-dog for a walk
And pick up the telephone.

Reading Kinsella in the Brasserie While the Wife Is Doing Her Hair

What am I doing here
Reading Kinsella in the brasserie
While the wife is doing her hair?

Later I'll mosey to Montmartre
And join the poets in Place du Tertre;
And then maybe I'll go to Chartres
And take a photo of the glass
(Will I say a prayer?)
I'm reading Kinsella in the brasserie
While the wife is doing her hair.

I turn the pages absently
Reading Kinsella in the brasserie
In my head a dream of whores –
I ravish them, they ravish me
Reading Kinsella in the brasserie
While the wife is doing her hair.

And every day I sip cold beer
Turning pages sitting here
Framed again in the windowpane
While the wife is doing her hair.

The *serveuse*, smiling, seems to say to me
'Why are you alone in the brasserie?'
Oh, I'd tell her I don't care.
I'd buy her a beer or a Burgundy

And I wouldn't be alone in the brasserie
(Perhaps we'd go upstairs).

But I'm reading Kinsella in the brasserie
While the wife is doing her hair.

Garden

for Brenda

We were a garden dug by eager hands;
Weeds were swept by shovels underground;
Brown earth, blackened and split by winter,
Was picked to a skeleton by starving birds.

Spring surprised us with a yelp of daisies
Defiant as a terrier guarding his home ground;
We planted seed in the cleft of drills
Slimy with earthworms.

Today I picked the first fruit of our garden –
Bloody with earth, I offered it to you;
You washed it and anointed it,
We ate it like viaticum.

In the eating of pith and seed
I loved you.

Rain

1
She was a bearded woman
Living alone.
Her mother stole milk from churns
In a dry year with *piseogs*
They said
And crossed themselves
Who revered the Devil
And feared God.

There's no luck in *piseogs*:
Look at her mad sons
Locked in 'Beauty's Home'.
They were run down
Through furze and river
After the mother's funeral
And committed to asylum until death.
Crows attacked her coffin
As dusty earth
Crumbled in the open grave.

To save the farm, they said,
Her daughter had the boys impounded.

She was the randy one –
'Wide as a wellington'.
Only broken bachelors
Would straddle the bearded woman
In the hollow field
And even that was before the funeral.

2
He was oak,
Watered well in darkness
And in light.
Sprouting, he was a delight –
Strong of trunk and branch.
Birds twittered from his breast.

The storm was drought
In the wailing night.
In the wind
He stood upright.
He was oak.
Lightning convulsed his brain.

Still oak
But splintered
He wandered through his people.
They ran from his twisted fire
And pain:
He had known the storm,
Had cursed it,
Called it brother.

Piety crossed itself again.

3
No song danced from his branches.
No bird nested in her hedge.

The fire saw no evil
But piety pledged vengeance.

Prayer
Was wagtails in the morning
After storm.

The bearded woman whispered
In the twisted branches
Her lamenting strain.
His pain entered her.

It rained.

piseogs: witchcraft, sorcery

from Road to the Horizon

(1987)

Poem for Brenda

I
The White Page

1
With love inarticulate as the draft
Revised
Despaired of

Revised
Crossed

Lover to lover cannot say
His deepest words.

And the white page beckons
Like a poacher's light
And words break cover
As the fight begins
On the periphery of sense
Where meaning lingers
And word ends.

2
Then silence.
The battle over.

We return to decipher in this spent rage
The voices that were voiceless
Of the words we twisted shapeless,

To lay out the carnage

On the marble of the page
Till sound and sense agree

Redeemed in this arrangement,
This obituary.

II
A Language

'Lover to lover cannot say
His deepest words'
Are my words
And half-true.

But love finds the voices
That lurk behind the clichés.

Now words regress
To repossess some vast, sunny Eden of youth
Where a child can tell his child lover
A childish truth
And games of love and hate
Are created articulate.

Now the sap is rising
Thick as dew –

In or out of this garden
I can never lie to you
Though a language compromises truth.

III
Another Language

With you

I am husband,
Singer,
Poet
Forever sounding words for truth.

I edge beyond the edges of my depth
Returning always safely
(Next time to be swept?) –
The road to the horizon has no end.

There are times when you call words from me like sperm.

And together we have sounded the pristine words
Until our mouths together are one tongue
And sense has woken to its language
And all the nameless impulses of brain
Flow towards understanding.

And I salute you, Brenda with 'Brenda hello'
Where our native tongue would bless you
And so
Because we know the silent understanding
I bring new words to you, Brenda,
Once again.

A Game of Forty-one

Tonight it's forty-one:
Pay to your right, 10p a man.
Doubles a jink, and play your hand.
If you renege, we'll turn you.

Yes, tonight it's forty-one:
A table for six, any pub in town.
Follow suit, and stand your round.
If you renege, we'll turn you.

Tonight it's forty-one
And tomorrow in the Dáil
Fine Gael and Fianna Fáil
Debate their Bill –

'Cos on the television
They're talking of revision
And extension of detention
And extra Special Powers.

So we sit here hour by hour
Getting drunk on special Power:
A game of cards at night now
Costs more and more and more.

And you trump hard on the table,
And you pay up when you're able.
If you don't, then you're in trouble –
It's worse than to renege.

Oh, it's always forty-one:
Play your cards at work, at home –

Even sitting on a barstool
They won't let you alone.

Yes, it's always forty-one,
And I'm really in the dumps
For the horse-mouth at my elbow
Has just led the ace of trumps.

And I'm playing forty-one
And wishing there were some
Other way of spending
A lifetime in this town.

But the poet and the priest –
Beauty and the Beast –
Must all sit down together
And cut this common deck.

And there is no Bill or Bible
But the verdict of the table
And the argument of players
To dispute the point of rule.

So tonight it's forty-one
And tomorrow, next week, next month,
And I'm out if I suggest
Another rule.

We'll turn you: We'll put you out of this round of cards

Parting

Past is past
And loving ends –
And meeting thus
We're old friends.

As loving ends
When past is past,
Here at her funeral
We're friends at last.

And the coffin slips
Through the church door
Like the love of lovers
Who were nothing more.

For past is past
And love is changed
And behind her coffin
We speak again.

With the shovels parting
The black earth for her,
We part again
This living squalor.

Hunting the Wren

for Desmond and Olda FitzGerald

> The Wren, the Wren, the king of all birds,
> Saint Stephen's Day he was caught in the furze
> So up with the kettle and down with the pan
> And give us a penny to bury the Wren.
> *– Traditional rhyme*

The villages of Ireland have lost their tongue
And ritual descends to custom
For custom to become some conservation,
Some parody of the spirit.

The romp of spirit, the riot of soul
Is pathetic when ritual lacks a role.
And so, the Christmas over, we hunt the Wren
But the hunt assumes no meaning.

We are the flower of that which died before us
And if we do not know what died, or why it died,
We walk in darkness.

Who would hunt the Wren must first let darkness in.
We will have inherited our ancestry
If the symbol is within.

Symbol of a mystic people is the Wren
On the march of the imagination.

So let us go in darkest winter to hunt the Wren
With skin of goat that was sacrificed for a drum,
With the Wren totem on the holly bush.
Masked, let all the village come

With rattle of bones and hoofbeat of *bodhrán*,
With music to charm the spirit of the Wren,
With dancing to express the form of music,
With the archaic pageant ordered in a song
For this is the truth of Wrenboys
And we must pass it on
In the carnival of darkness,
Singers of the sun.

Bodhrán: a traditional goatskin drum

Keeper

for my father

First
My father mowing –
Turning an early spring
Into a green lawn.

And again
A sun of daisy and dandelion –

My father mows the lawn.

Then
My father weeding
Daisy and dandelion,
Patient fingers
Perennial with white slime –

My father:
Keeper of his lawn,
His mind.

The Poet's Garden

There's a pollen of bees
In the heart of the flowers

A survival of grubs
In the cabbage

A compost of words
At one end of the plot

At the other
A stillbirth of garbage.

from Dancing Through
(1990)

Predator

for Vincent Buckley

Within the woods, the coolness of the sea.
The lesser birds and songbirds all have fled.
Fern, dock and nettle bend before me,
But I have lost the ancient lore of herbs.

The undergrowth is barbed, a fence of brambles,
And I have come to feed on wilderness;
Like fur, these bits of human where I stumbled
Are tugged by rooks and jackdaws for their nests.

Bleakness of woods dying under ivy –
Here a tree, moss-splintered, home of lice;
Here a branch whose shoots have burst, divided
From lichened bark: bud-red grows branchlet-bright.

As if the crows could turn away the stranger,
They wheel their frantic chainsaw-song of fright.
Crows in the crow dominion sense the danger:
The flightless beast looks up, protects his eyes.

The Spider and the Fly

for D. J. Enright

Won't you come into my parlour,
Says the spider to the fly.
You can't deny me:
Effort is useless against me.

I am anarchic as imagination
And treacherous as sex;
I am stronger than your will.
Come into my parlour.

Here slave is master,
Master slave.
In this parlour
Is all you crave.
Here wounds open
That were healed:
Here all secrets
Are revealed.
Come into my parlour.

You strain against me
But I own your brain.
You should have learned
That I possess you.
Again and again
You pull against me
To no avail.
Try as you will to root me out
You'll fail.

Regale me.
Sing: *Hail spider!*

Hail! All hail!
The spider is all-powerful
Where you are frail.

Come into my parlour,
Says the spider to the fly.
Do not deny your nature.
Accept that you're a creature
Subservient to me.

Accept
And fly and spider
Will agree
For the spider is in you
As the fly is part of me.

*

I am spider
I am fly –
That much I can't deny

And I have tried
To maintain that great divide

But why?

If the spider and the fly
Are one already,
I must open up my parlour.

Oh fly that lacks a spider
Oh spider that lacks a fly
Come into my parlour –

Softly I.

Virgin Rock, Ballybunion

for Johnny Coolahan

Surrounded by breakers,
I stand
Where the grinding ocean
Turns weakness into sand.
I approach my true shape,
Being weathered –
Cliff to rock to strand . . .

In the Midst of Possibility

Now I love you
Free of me:
In this loving I can see
The *You* of you
Apart from me –
The *You* of you that's ever free.

This is the *You* I love.
This is the *You* I'll never have.
This is the *You* beyond possession –

The *You* that's ever true
While ever changing,
Ever new.

Now,
Naked,
Free,
The *You* of you
Meets the *Me* of me
And to see is to love,
To love, to see:

In the midst of possibility
We agree.

The Pregnant Earth

for Győző Ferencz

The hurt was there before me,
Inherent in my genes;

The hurt was all around me
And I heard;

The hurt drove one to suicide,
Stripped another's nerves,
And turned one to singing.

*

And I became a singer –
My songs flew wild and free,
But the hurt's gravity tethered them
As it had tethered me.

And I became a cave-man
Groping in my soul,
Hacking at obstruction
For light to fill the hole
Till my eyes became bats' eyes
And I found my way through echoes
In the dark.

*

The pregnant earth,
Midwinter,
Sings its song to me,

Humming in its belly:
Arise, Persephone . . .

This simple song sustains me
As the darkness claims its dead –

O light within the darkness,
O carol in my head . . .

from The Father's Part

(1992)

Presentation

On Christmas Eve
We present our child
(Adopted after all these years)
First
In the ancestral home.

Tom, *paterfamilias*,
Kisses him.

This is the floor
Tom's father crawled,
My father crawled.

Mary,
Woman of the house,
Coaxes him across the floor.

Now
You're a Fitzmaurice

And in this ancestral home
With cousins,
Aunts and uncles
You are welcome;

For you're our new communion –
The family receive
As Mary pours a health to you
On this first Christmas Eve.

Ties

'Son'
I call you
And the name possesses:

What the Board made legal,
The word makes true.

Your first 'Da-da',
My first 'Son'
Have named our recognition.

Later
You may venture on your own
Seeking
What even this love can't give.

No matter:

We inhabit our appellations,
'Daddy'
'Son',
Part of each other's language . . .

This will live.

Eden

He knocks the shampoo in the bath –
His look asks
'Is this wrong or right?'

I commend his naive act.

Puzzled by his action
My son makes God of me,
Remains a child in Eden
Till he eats of every tree.

*

Adam was right to eat the apple –

He was utterly unfree,
Kept,
A child in Eden.

He'd have left the garden anyway
With his wife and kids
Moral only in his freedom.

*

I slice an apple for my son,
Give it him to eat;

He bites it,
Then grimaces –

Finds it sour
But sweet.

Art

You sprawl on the floor
Scribbling on an invoice
Ignoring *Tom and Jerry* on TV.

'I make it! I write the picture!'
You divert me, imploring
'That's John's picture'.

I let you be.

Then
'Up Daybo's lap!',
You dance and tug me.

'No John!
Daybo's writing poems' –

A pause . . .

'John write a pone! John write a pone!',
You barter.

Your ploy shines on refusal
And it thaws.

Sitting on my lap
You grab my biro,
Cover Daybo's draft about you
With your scrawl –

'That's Daybo's pone', you beam,
'Dirty! Dirty!'

Inherent in creation is its fall.

An Only Child No Longer

John, tomorrow you'll have a sister –
How's that going to affect you? And me?
Your Daybo'll become 'Da-da' to his daughter
And I'll be no longer yours exclusively.

John, forgive me this betrayal –
Though we've drawn 'John's baby', I fear you'll see it thus
When Nessa cries and captures all attention
And you hide your face prostrate in a fuss.

Tonight you're monarch of your kingdom
Where everything is 'John's' that you can grab.
Tomorrow you must share, and I must teach you
Who healed me with your childhood and your gab.

from The Village Sings

(1996)

Hence the Songs

In memoriam *Billy Cunningham, singer*

How soon great deeds are abstract . . .

Hence the songs –
The mighty deeds the tribe sings in the bar:
Gaisce diminished by the video.

Men I never knew still star
In North Kerry Finals,
Their deeds not history but myth,
Alive upon a singer's breath;

Again local men are martyred
In a lonely glen;

Now love is lost,
A Rose is won –

Things insufficient till they're sung . . .

Gaisce: (Irish) valour, great exploits, boasting

Gaeilge

for Micheál Ó Conghaile

I was wild and wonderful
With many dialects –
Erratic, individual
As the genius that expressed

Itself through me;
On my terms suitors wooed –
I revealed to those who pleased me
My hidden voice and mood.

I was queen of dialect
And language through me sang
Like poetry, the thrill
Of words upon my tongue.

I gave myself to language –
We agreed like rhyme,
Different, yet harmonious.
Widowed now by time,

Dependent on the grammar
Prescribed for me – this crutch,
Doctored by officials
Who care about as much

For wilderness and wonder
As a civil servant's form,
Oh for the tongue of passion!
To be swept again by storm!

Gaeilge: the Irish language

The Common Touch

for Robert McDowell

Perky Nolan was a stuck-up dog –
The schoolmaster's.
He never fought with the other dogs that held the street.
He was manicured as street-urchins would never be.

Perky went for walkies with the master's daughter,
Manicured as herself.
Beside her, Perky tiptoed like a dancer;
He cocked his leg, important as the Anthem in Croke Park;
He cocked his nose, a mammy's boy,
And broadcast with his bark.

Perky was all the things a villager would never be,
And so the village waited.

One day Perky got loose and walked free;
The village nosed him.
Perky made a show of baring teeth,
But there was no harm in him.

This was the chance we'd waited for.

'Perky! Here boy! Here boy!
Good dog! Good dog!'
We called, holding out our hands.
Perky sniffed and padded towards us.

'Kick the shit out of him boys', we exploded.

Shoes, boots, wellingtons and bare toes thudded into him.
He howled and ran.

'That'll teach him to put on airs', the village gloated.

Perky found the common touch –
The same for dog and man.

Ode to a Bluebottle

It never is quite summer
Till you fizz around the room,
Drone to summer's chanter,
Spurt, a loosed balloon.

It never is quite summer
Till you're splattered on the sill:
Oh, we don't want all of summer.
Much of it we kill.

Willie Dore

Willie Dore was simple,
He smelled. The village fool,
He lived alone among the rats
In a shack below the school.

Two rats' eyes in his leather face
Stabbed out beneath the layer
Of dirt that blackened him like soot.
He wasn't born *quare*,

But some disease the doctor
Couldn't cure (or name)
Trapped him in his childhood,
Hobbling his brain.

Willie Dore was a happy man
Though peevish as a huff –
He fed, he drank, he slept, he rose,
He dreamed – that was enough . . .

Each sausage scrounged from a travelling van
Was a vital victory;
Each penny coaxed from a passing priest
Was a cunning comedy.

Willie never knew his age –
No matter how you'd pry,
'The one age to Mary Mack'
Was all he could reply.

He lived as he imagined,
Saw manna in the street,
Eighty years of scavenging,
Admitting no defeat.

Quare: a version of 'queer' meaning 'strange', 'unusual', 'mentally unbalanced'

The Village Hall

The old hall with its shaky stage
Was good enough for us –
Bill Horan and Eileen Manaher
Wholly marvellous

As they called up here before us
A world of their own,
The magic I have grown to love,
The farce I loved, outgrown.

The queue outside the musty hall,
The key turned in the lock,
The stampede to the benches,
The fizz, the sweets, clove rock;

And then the silence as the play
Took us in its spell,
Local folk turned gods and queens
In this miracle.

The hall is old, not worth repair,
They'll knock it, build anew;
My boy and girl will taste in there
The magic that I knew;

They'll find the things a village finds
In the local hall –
That as Eileen becomes a queen
We're not ourselves at all.

Fireplace

Where nothing was
But space alone
A fireplace is
Revealed in stone

Which shapes and garlands
The hearth's void –
The empty centre.
With what pride

The mason smiles
Who has let be
The perfect
Possibility.

Port na bPúcaí

for Tony Mac Mahon

'Music of the Fairies' –
I wonder what he knew:
He heard a world and named it;
Came back to tell it, too.

Possessed by so-called 'fairies',
The fiddler had to find
A beauty that would please him
As they played upon his mind.

'Music of the Fairies' –
Like any poet he knew
That beauty would destroy him
Unless he made it, too.

Port na bPúcaí: (Irish) 'The Fairies' Music', a Blasket Island air. It was believed to have been heard from the fairies and translated to the fiddle by a Blasket fiddler. It has been suggested that the air is based on the call of a seal (or a whale) heard that night off Inis Icíleáin, the most southerly of the Blaskets.

Mary

Hail, full of grace . . .
The Angel, uninvited
Came to you in your own place
And your word united

Heaven and Earth, Above, Below –
God needed you to say
Behold Thy handmaid; had you said *No*,
Where was God today?

A plucky girl, unmarried too
At the time of this conception –
What some would do to such as you
Does not bear mention.

You took your chance on God and life
No man before your will,
Queen of Heaven, common wife
No precious, pale religious thing,
No prop for those who would
Impose themselves on everything
Not least your womanhood.

'I Thirst'

Midnight Mass one Christmas Eve,
The Parish comes to pray –
A midnight of nostalgia
After a hard day;

For some have been preparing
Their Christmas at the sink,
And others have spent the day
Revelling in drink.

At Midnight Mass, the Parish
Bows its head in prayer –
All but one have come along
In pious posture there.

All day, he's been drinking
In the Corner House;
When it comes to closing time
He buys, to carry out
For after Mass, two bottles
Of Guinness Extra Stout.

And he stands there with the others
At the back wall of the church;
When it comes to the Offertory,
Suddenly with a lurch

He staggers up the centre aisle
While the crowd looks on in shock,
Halting at the altar rails,
Careful not to drop

The bottles, he takes them out,
Plants them on the rails,
Faces the congregation,
Waves and then repairs

To the back and anonymity,
Hitches up his arse,
And some are shocked, and some amused
At his unholy farce.

But the Christ who thirsts on Calvary
Has waited all these years
For a fellow cursed with the cross of thirst
To stand him these few beers.

Good Friday

Good Friday was the day of periwinkles:
The only day we got them – oh the treat!
An old lady and her son came up from Bally
With an assload. They were much more fun than meat.

They sold them by the handful to us children;
We took them home and pestered Mom for pins.
They looked like snots when you fished them out. But Jesus!
That was some way to atone for all your sins!

We ate them by the fistful all that morning,
Receiving the essence of the tide.
The empty shells prefigured eggs for Easter.
At three o'clock the Christ was crucified.

The tang of winkles flavours my Good Fridays,
The emptiness familiar as the day.
The old woman's dead, her son too. Every weekend
The winkle man revives them on his tray.

In Memoriam Danny Cunningham,
1912–1995

I take her to the funeral home –
She wants to see him dead;
She's not afraid – she rubs his hands
And then explores his head.

'He not wake up I rub him.
Look Daddy! He not move.
Where Danny, Dad?' she asks me.
'Danny's dead, my love.'

'Where Danny, Dad', she asks again;
Then suddenly it's clear –
'The old Danny in the box', she says;
'The new one – he not here'.

Oisín's Farewell to Niamh

No one can live forever
And even if we could
We'd choose death in the long run.
This is good.

Tír na nÓg's for children –
Nothing changes there,
Everyone always smiling,
Flowers in their hair;

And all their songs are child's songs
Where nothing ever grows,
But to a poet and soldier,
To such a one as knows

The death-and-birth of seasons,
Though Eternal Youth's his bride,
Such a one must live his life,
Such a one can't hide

In eternal youth and happiness
Where nothing ever dies –
Once you've lived with mortals,
Tír na nÓg is lies.

So fare thee well, my princess,
I must leave you now, my dear,
Back to death in Ireland
To face my fear.

Tír na nÓg: (Irish) The Land of Eternal Youth

A Bedtime Story

I want to give my children what I got –
A sign of middle age and childhood past:
'A story about Daddy – tell us what
You did when you were little – just like us'.
What survives our childhood we don't choose –
We must forgive our childhood if we can:
We cannot cite our childhood as excuse –
Hurt is not a licence to do wrong.
And so I bring my children to my past,
A past that was unhappy as 'twas good –
A story now, and so my kids have guessed
The happy ending, as indeed they should.
I tuck them in as sleep tugs at their lids.
I hope they'll wish their childhood on their kids.

May Dalton

The last word that was left to her was 'honour',
The stroke had taken all the rest away,
The one thing the void could not take from her
Was herself, and so she used to say
'Honour! Honour! Honour!' when you addressed her,
'Honour! Honour! Honour!' while her hand
Clutched her agitation. What depressed her
Was how those closest failed to understand
'Honour! Honour! Honour!', how our beaming
Was the beaming of an adult at a child:
'Honour! Honour! Honour!' had no meaning
For any but May Dalton. So we smiled.
A single word held all she had to say;
Enclosed within this word, she passed away.

To Martin Hayes, Fiddler

All that we are given, we can use;
All the notes are there for us to praise –
The tune's set out before us, yet *we* choose:
The tune evolves in playing. Martin Hayes
Susses out each note before he cues
It. Taking thought, he chooses what it says,
Weaves into the fabric his own news:
The tune's predestined, not the way he plays.

The music *is*, the fiddler's taken thought –
All our moments lead to this last *doh*,
All the options, everything that's sought:
What we hear that's played is what we know.
Holy! Holy! Holy! what is wrought!
He raises up, rubs rosin to the bow.

from A Wrenboy's Carnival

(2000)

Sonnet to Brenda

I won't compare you to a summer's day,
The beaches all deserted in the rain –
Some way, this, to spend a holiday
(You're sorry now you didn't book for Spain).
No! The weather can't be trusted in these parts –
It's fickle as a false love's said to be;
I could get sentimental about hearts
But that's not my style. Poetry,
The only thing that's constant in my life,
The only thing I know that still is true
As my love remains for you, dear wife –
This, then, is what I'll compare to you.
The iambic heart that pulses in these lines
Measures out my love. And it still rhymes.

Gaeltacht

Here, for once, I didn't pine for home:
This was a world where language altered all;
Here Irish fitted like a poem –
In school, 'twas just a subject; here you'd fall
In love with being Irish: you were free
To learn the words of love not taught in school;
Oh! Irish was that girl at the *céilí* –
If you could only ask her out, not make a fool
Of yourself, and dance with her all night,
You'd learn the moods of Irish on her tongue;
She smiled at you, and oh! your head was light,
You danced with her and wheeled and waltzed and swung.
We danced all night, we didn't even kiss,
But this was love, was Irish, and was bliss.

Gaeltacht: (Irish) an Irish-speaking district; the state of being Irish
céilí: (Irish) an Irish-dancing session

A Parent's Love

How close the sound of laughter and of tears!
My children watching *Dumbo* on TV
In the next room – are those wails or cheers?
At this remove their screaming worries me.

Do my children laugh or cry in the next room?
I check them out, and this is what I see –
No light illuminates the falling gloom,
Instead of watching *Dumbo* on TV,

High jinks on the sofa – they're both well,
I tick them off, their giggles fill and burst;
A parent's love knows all it needs of hell –
I hear them play and strangely fear the worst.

In the Attic

You're going up in the attic, Dad –
Please can I come too?
I'll even get the ladder, Dad,
And put it up for you.

Of all the places in our house
I love the attic best;
It's dark there – dark as Christmas
With every box a chest

Of surprise and promise –
The things we store up there
Are put away like memories
To open if you dare.

You're going up in the attic, Dad –
Can I come up too, *please*!
For hidden in the attic
Among the memories

Is part of me and part of you –
The part we seldom show;
Oh, up there in the attic, Dad,
Is all we're not, below.

Listening to *Desperados Waiting for a Train*

for John

How one thing always leads us to another!
I see you with your grandad once again
As you walk off from your father and your mother
To join him in the world of grown-up men.
And yes, son, local folk called you his sidekick
As you walked around the village hand in hand,
No baby-talk, 'twas adult stuff like politics
And it felt good to be treated like a man.
And though grandad's dead and everything is changing,
And you're growing up and soon will leave us, son,
And life's a past we're always rearranging,
When the kid walks with his hero in that song
I see you with your grandad once again
As you walk away to join the world of men.

A Wrenboy's Farewell

for Maurice Heffernan and the Moyvane Wrenboys

Farewell to winter madness, summer larks,
The show is over, we're back on firm land;
No more our torches will light up the dark,
The time has come and now we must disband.
Farewell to music, singing, dancing, rhymes,
The public show of all we are about,
This pageant that we dreamed in other times –
The show is over. Put the torches out.
The old are weary, wise in their defeat,
The young protest and wonder if they can
Revive the glory, again march down the street
Under the proud banner of Moyvane.
Go home. The show is over. The banner's furled.
We walk back up the street into the world.

Batt Mannon

Batt Mannon is our hamster,
Spends all his time awake
Gnawing at his cage bars
Attempting to escape.

But steel will not be broken
By the strongest jaws,
And yet he keeps on trying.
Is this because

The hamster has no memory,
Or, too stupid to give in,
He's torn by no depression,
Hope his greatest sin?

Whatever – he keeps gnawing
Till pity frees him for
A few hard-earned minutes
To run around the floor.

He understands no pity.
The hamster is his jaws –
He thinks they've won him freedom.
This is his reward.

He gnaws the bars that hold him
All his hours awake.
Only we who pity
Know there's no escape.

The Well

I heard it of a winter's night
In childhood, years ago
When tales were told to keep the cold
Outside with the wind and snow

How once upon a moonlit night
A piper passed this way
Coming from a *céilí*
In the parish of Athea

And as he walked he whistled
A tune, a merry tune
And the only other sound that night
Was howling at the moon.

He walked along the fairy path
Whistling his merry tune
When suddenly a darkness
Stole across the moon

And all the dogs fell silent
As he came upon the well
And a voice from the waters spoke to him
And this is what befell:

There's some call it glaucoma
And some the fairies' curse
For when he woke next morning
Beside the fairy bush

He was blind; and ever after
He would never tell

What the voice of the waters whispered
From the fairy well.

The fairies are no longer
And all their wanton harm,
And the well supplies fresh water
Piped up to a farm,

And when I ask the old man
Who told the tale to me
If he believes in fairies
He says, 'I don't believe

In fairies',
And turns to face me then:
'No! I don't believe in fairies.
But I'm afraid of them'.

Geronimo

for Kathleen Cain

Here, *tiswin* and Apaches didn't mix –
The White Eyes banned its brewing, just in case:
Drunk, Apaches could be lunatics,
They'd get out of their heads and wreck the place –
The place the White Eyes sent them when they took
Their land, their homes, their way of life to live
As the White Eyes told them – by *their* book.
Geronimo got drunk; a fugitive,
He jumped the reservation with his band
(He broke the law, and soon would pay the price),
Returned to his home, familiar land –
Sober, perhaps, he'd have considered twice,
Ignored a truth; but, drunk, Geronimo,
A warrior again, knew he should go.

tiswin: Apache corn beer

Ode to a Pint of Guinness

'*An Buachaill Caol Dubh*', 'The Blonde in the Black Skirt' –
You have given me life which I'd never have known,
For I was the shy one, inward and lonesome,
Fearful of people the years I was growing.

You came to me first in the years I was courting –
No girl would stay with me on lemonade;
You gave me fine words and a high reputation
For romance and laughter. At last I was made!
You came to me sad and you came to me happy –
There were parts of myself that lay unexplored,
But thanks to you, Guinness, there's nothing within us
That doesn't come out in thought, deed or word.

There are two kinds of truth, one drunk and one sober –
The ancient Egyptians knew this very well;
Before they'd pronounce, they'd examine it both ways –
The kind of good counsel I'd bottle and sell.

How different my life would be measured without you –
An egghead, I fear, with his nose in a book;
But now I can scan the pulse of my people
And the scholars will read it to get one last look
At the village before it has lost its own story,
The last place on earth for the wild and the free,
'Ere we turn to designer beers, beautiful bodies,
And we speak like bad actors speak on TV.

So here's to you, Guinness, muse and confuser –
You brought me to visions, you brought me to fart:

All the pain that you caused me was nothing at all, love,
To the knowledge you taught to this once-sober heart!

An Buachaill Caol Dubh: (Irish) 'The Dark Slender Boy', a synonym for alcohol from the song of the same name by Seán Aerach Ó Seanacháin (mid-eighteenth century).

The Woman of the House

The village – Ballygariff
Sometime in the past
Where the clock advanced for Closing Time
Is the only thing that's fast.

In her pub, Maggie Browne
(Browne's her maiden name)
Serves pints and whiskies to a group
Who've recently come home

On holiday from England,
They wear their Sunday best –
They're out to prove that exile
Does better than the rest

Who stay at home in Bally
And work that windswept hill
And so they dress in Sunday best
And flash big twenty bills.

Enter then Tom Guiney,
The singer, for a beer;
He's bought tobacco for himself,
Sugar, tea and flour

For his wife above in Barna,
He comes in for 'just the one'
But the exiles stand him porter
And demand of him a song.

All afternoon he sings for them;
At 'The Home I Left Behind'

The exiles back in Bally
Stare into black pints

For song is all that's left them
Of Bally long ago,
The past is all that's left them,
The only home they know.

Tom Guiney, man of honour,
Will stand his round,
Though what's left in his pocket
Would hardly make a pound.

Nonetheless he calls for
A drink for the company –
'Twould never be said in Bally
He drank all day for free.

Maggie Browne sets up the drinks
And Tom must now admit
That he hasn't enough to pay for them –
Could she put it on the slate?

She does. And on with singing
But Maggie bides her time
And in a private moment
Takes Tom aside.

'Tom', she says, 'You'll never
Call for a drink again
With no money in your pocket
For a crowd like them.

'Call for your drink, Tom Guiney,
And when I put it up

If you've no money in your pocket
Let them take a sup

'Or two and let them talk
And then come up to me
And ask me for the change
Of the fiver you gave me;

'And Guiney, boy, you'll get it –
Never, never again
Let on that you've no money
To a crowd like them.'

The village – Ballygariff.
Time – the present. Now
We come to bury Maggie Browne;
We take and drink our stout –

We do this in memory
Of a woman we well know,
Exalter of the humble
In a singer long ago.

My People

1 Jimmy Nolan

Jimmy Nolan, grocer, typed my name,
The printed word, just like it was in books;
Back then, the printed word was fame,
I'd hold it up and look, and look, and look.
He took photos, too, of weddings around here,
Anything to earn an honest bob
(A wooden leg, his walk a little queer),
He'd show the snaps to Mam – another job
Well done, he courted praise ('twas all he sought);
He wrote the local *Notes*, and that was power,
He made the news from stories that were brought
By locals who would purchase tea and flour.
He typed us up, and every week we'd scan
Our inch of glory in *The Kerryman*.

2 Billy Cunningham

He told me that my singing was the equal
Of a goat pissing into a tin can.
Dismissed in youth! The story has a sequel –
He gave me songs when I grew a man,
The old songs that he learned from local rhymers
Who sang their place in triumph and defeat;
I'd spend evenings by his range with that old-timer
And all who cared to drop in from the street.
Sitting there in Uncle Billy's kitchen
Where neighbours walked once more beyond the grave
And youngsters smoked first fags and spoke of mitching
As Billy took out his teeth to sing a stave,

The past would come alive upon his breath.
In circles such as these there is no death.

3 'Old Jack Fitz'

'Old Jack Fitz', my Grandad, was a stern
Lover of perfection in his work.
His family, from early on, would learn
To harvest all their springs and never shirk.
They got on well in England and the States;
They danced their way through London in the war;
Their children come to Ireland, we're best mates:
I sing the old songs for them in the bar –
The songs his fellow farmers nightly sang
When Grandad and Nano would open up
Their *céilí* house and all the rafters rang
As neighbours came to sing and dance and sup
Where a lover of perfection could relax
Knowing the hay was saved, the oats in stacks.

4 Dad

A man before his time, he cooked and sewed,
Took care of me – and Mammy in her bed,
Stayed in by night and never hit the road.
I remember well the morning she was dead
(I'd been living up in Arklow – my first job,
I hit the road in patches coming home),
He came down from her room, began to sob
'Oh Gabriel, Gabriel, Gabriel, Mam is gone'.
He held me and I told him not to cry
(I loved her too, but thought this not the place –
I went up to her room, cried softly 'Why?'
Then touched her head quite stiffly, no embrace).

Now when the New Man poses with his kid,
I think of all the things my father did.

5 Mam

My mother wrote the meanings of hard words
In the margins of the books she'd recommend;
I coasted through those stories, and was stirred
By fantasy and romance: I'd pretend
To be what I was reading, made my bike
A cowboy horse, a hurley for a gun,
Picked a branch of hazel for a Viking
Spear; I'm sure she wondered at her son
Living out a fiction she'd prepared;
Her intention was to educate –
To spare me from a shop where if you dared
To speak your mind, customers might 'migrate'.
A grocer's wife, wary of romance,
She bought those books, and I should take my chance.

6 Mick

Looking at your photo as a boy,
I see you now at eighty still unbowed,
That couldn't-care-less look still in your eye,
The kind of look that stands out from the crowd.
That photo shows a soul who'd travel light,
Who'd never bind himself to any school,
Whose only use for money – that he might
Enjoy a drink with friends upon a stool.

Uncle Mick, you're all I'll never be,
You have no need of what the world can give;
A bachelor, you live with family,

In England all those years you lived in digs.
Home for you is simply what you are,
Who never owned a house or drove a car.

7 The Sandhills of Yamboorah

'By the Sandhills of Yamboorah', a book I read
When I was twelve or thirteen, 'way back when
I'd take a book and sneak off into bed
And read all day of heroes – mostly men.
But this was different: the pace was easy, slow –
As Australia itself, or so I guessed;
The boy (he wasn't named) just seemed to know
His time, his place were suited to him best.
Australia! where no Lancelot would roam,
Just an old black man who helped the boy with chores –
Much the same as the life I led at home,
A life which, some complain, is stagnant, bores.
I read that book; in time I'd learn to say
The heroes live beside me, day by day.

In Memory of My Mother

My mother lived for books though nearly blind.
An invalid, she read while she could see.
The only pleasure left her was her mind.

The books she read that pleased her were designed
To strip her life down to a clarity.
My mother lived for books though nearly blind

While I'd read all the comics I could find;
Confined to bed, she'd read 'good books' to me.
The only pleasure left her was her mind.

Delighting in the vision of her kind,
That second sight, the gift of poetry,
My mother lived for books though nearly blind,

Books I read from bookshelves that were lined
With poems she'd recite from memory.
The only pleasure left her was her mind.

And I remembered as I launched and signed
The first slim *Poems* of my maturity
How Mammy lived for books though nearly blind,
The only pleasure left to her, her mind.

So What if There's No Happy Ending?

In memoriam *Michael Hartnett*

So what if there's no happy ending?
Don't be afraid of the dark;
Open the door into darkness
And hear the black dogs bark.

Oh what a wonder is darkness!
In it you can view
The moon and stars of your nature
That daylight hid from you.

Open the door into darkness,
There's nothing at all to fear –
Just the black dogs barking, barking
As the moon and stars appear.

God Bless the Child

God bless the child that never grew to life,
Our dead embryo – not even a stillbirth –
Detached inside its mother's womb. My wife
And I can't even give it to the earth
From which life comes, returning it to dust.
I'll light a candle for it; on second thought,
I won't. I can't – to do so would be just
A sentimental gesture, a bouquet bought
At Reception on visiting my wife,
A silent touch perhaps to bring relief;
No candles then, I seek the words of life
That one, perhaps, might fertilise our grief.
Now every word upon my lips is prayer
Pregnant with the life that we must bear.

Requiescat

He shouldered Mammy's coffin
And I was at his side,
A strong man in his fifties;
More than Mammy died

As we lowered her coffin,
My childhood ended then
As I stood beside my father
At her grave among the men.

We shouldered other coffins
These twenty years and more,
My father strong and steady
Though our shoulders would be sore.

And even last October
When his sister Nora died,
At eighty years he shouldered her
Still steady by my side.

He shouldered no more coffins –
When my aunt Mary died
And we went to lift her coffin,
My father stood aside.

His hand upon her coffin,
He followed up the aisle,
My father still beside me
Awhile.

His brothers now too feeble
To lift his coffin when

My father died, we wheeled him,
Myself and those old men.

And as we lowered you, father,
A generation knew
That the time had come for passing on.
Now I inherit you.

In the Woods

'X' on a tree trunk
Marks no buried treasure here
Children wonder why

*

A rotting tree stump
In the middle of the woods
Mushrooms with new life

*

Where there are nettles
There are dock leaves to heal us
In a spot nearby

Big Con

for my dear friend Con Greaney, singer

Big Con lives in the mountain
In a thatched house on his own,
His wife is dead fifteen years,
His family, long grown,

Have left the ancestral mountain
But Con will not remove:
His life is in the mountain,
His love.

Born on the mountain
These eighty years and more,
Not *born* so much as quarried;
The mountain life was poor

('Twas Rooska of the curlew),
But not poor of heart –
He came from singing people
Whose life was art.

Big Con, king of singers,
Has songs that only he
Brought from the singing people.
He sang his songs for me.

*

Once upon an emptiness
The Lost Man came home –
The man was lost because
He had lost his song.

He searched everywhere but couldn't find it
(Did he ever have the song?
He wondered)
So he collected songs.

He went to the oldest singers,
He learned all their songs,
He sang them for his people
But still did not belong.

One night, he sang with Donie Lyons,
A farmer out of Glin,
A flute player and singer.
Donie said to him:

'There's an old man in the west Limerick hills
That no one remembers now;
He might have what you're looking for'.
They finished their pints of stout;

They bought beer and whiskey
As an offering to Big Con
And drove into the mountain.
Would the giant sing his songs?

'Ye're welcome as the flowers of May',
Beamed Big Con, 'come in!
How're you keeping, Donie?
How're ye all in Glin?'

'Fine, Con', replied Donie;
'Con, I brought this man,
He's recorded many singers,
He's looking for a song'.
'If I have the song, he'll get it;
Make yereselves at home'.

We drank a few throws of whiskey,
Knocked back a couple of beers,
Then Con exploded into song.
The Lost Man, startled, hears

Him bend the air and twist it –
An old life made anew,
And every time 'twas different
And every time 'twas true,
The song that he was looking for,
The self that he once knew.

*

We break for beer and whiskey
And then return to song,
And song turns to story:
The story is Big Con . . .

'I remember my time in England,
Times were bad 'round here;
I had to leave my wife and children
In Rooska for a year.

I took the boat for England,
Met my brother at the quay –
He brought me home to Huddersfield,
Looked for work for me.

A few days I lived off him
And then one night he said
'There's a job going with the darkies –
I'd be careful of that crowd'.

But I worked away with the black men,

They were the same as me –
They found me strange, I found them strange;
We worked silently

Until one day my partner
Forgot to bring his lunch –
He was leaving the job at dinner hour
For what you'd now call 'brunch'.

'There's no need to go', I told him,
'I have plenty for us here';
I gave him half my sandwiches;
After work we went for beer.

And here was I – someplace –
Black men all around;
They stood to me all evening,
Wouldn't let me stand a round.

And what was it but a sandwich,
Pan loaf that made a friend?
They drove me home at closing time;
My brother was out of his mind:

'Jeezus, I thought they'd killed you –
In that place at night;
You don't know where you're going'.
'Them people is all right',

I told him.
'I'm welcome there, they said,
And the reason that I'm welcome
Is I gave a black man bread'.

And one day in the woollen mill,
A bale fell on my foot,

I was going to the doctor
But my partner said, 'No good! –

You no go to doctor,
Him take you off the job,
We do your work till you better,
You no lose a bob'.

So I turned up each morning
And the black men did my work,
We went for beer each evening
And I'd go home after dark.

And the night before I was leaving
I spent it with the blacks;
They were singing their songs
And one said in the jacks:

'Big Con, you have your own songs?'
I told him I could sing
But they wouldn't know my singing;
Still, they made me sing.

I sang the songs the mountain sang
At Feast and Fast and Fair
And d'you know, 'twas like the mountain
Had removed from here to there.

We drank all night, we said goodbye,
We'd never meet again;
I took the boat next evening,
Went back to bogs and drains.'

*

At peace at last, the Lost Man

Sent Con's songs throughout the land
And the legend grew with the singers
Who sought out this old man . . .

'There's a concert up in Dublin, Con;
Everyone will be there;
Will you come and sing your songs for us
Pure as mountain air?'

On the night of the big concert,
His first time so far from home
Since he returned from Huddersfield,
We gazed around our room

(I'd travelled to Dublin with him –
He needed me, he said;
He didn't know Dublin
And I did).

A hotel room, en suite, TV,
But Con got bored with that,
He took off downstairs to find the bar
For a pint, a pipe and chat.

Who is this old singer
They're putting on tonight?
An old man from the mountains.
Can he do it here? He might . . .

The MC shepherds Big Con
Backstage from the bar:
'Con', he chides, 'this is no pub,
This stage is for stars –

'You can't just start up singing,
You must talk first to the crowd;

Do you think, Con, you can do it?'
Con just laughs out loud –

'I see the Pope in Galway
When he said Mass on the TV –
He told the crowd he loved them;
Don't worry about me'.

'*Ladies and gentlemen, Big Con*' –
Silence, a polite clap,
And Con saunters out on stage
With his pint and cap.

He remembers the Pope in Galway
As he faces the dark hall –
'People of Dublin, I loves ye!'
The whole place is enthralled;

He sings six songs, his quota,
But the crowd cries out for more,
And when he's finished singing,
They clap till their hands are sore.

*

Big Con and the Lost Man
Travel home by train,
And the Lost Man says to Big Con,
'I won't see your like again'.

Over in the west Limerick hills
In a thatched house with his dog,
Big Con lives, a giant.
If his life was one hard slog

Now they come throughout the land
To learn at his feet –
'Ye're welcome as the flowers of May'
I hear an old man greet.

from I and the Village

(2002)

Aisling Gheal

One day back in the 'sixties
When everyone thought they were free
(Nothing that couldn't be done then) –
Everyone, that is, but me,

I was hitching a ride to the city
When a Zephyr pulled up by my side
And a vision in blonde hair and mini-skirt
Asked me did I want a ride.

I sat into the Zephyr beside her,
And, struck by her beauty, I fell
Silent beside my fast driver
Rehearsing what story to tell.

Would I talk of the Stones and the Beatles
And win her with music and lore
That I'd read up last week in the *Spotlight*,
Such tales as she'd want to hear more?

But what if she didn't like music?
What would we talk about then?
She talked of the troubles of Ireland
And the woes of her women and men;

And how England, that chauvinist England,
Was the cause of her trouble, but she
Would fight to the death for her freedom
And was counting on young men like me.

So I started to talk about England
But she railed they were barbarous boors

With no culture that any could speak of –
At least, no great culture like hers.

And she spoke of the Island of Scholars
And Saints who brought Europe to light,
And the chieftains and kings of Old Ireland
As eager in love as to fight;

And her poets who could charm with their verses,
And her bards who could soothe with their song,
And how England, that chauvinist England,
Had inflicted on her a great wrong.

And here was I squirming beside her,
Her mini-skirt driving me wild,
Torn between acquiescing
(For I was but lately a child)

And protesting the glories of England
(For, alas, I had read history)
Afraid that this beautiful vision
Would vanish forever from me.

Yes! I spoke of the glories of England
And she with a toss of her head
Cut off my history lesson:
'To hell with the Romans', she said.

'To hell with the Romans', she countered,
A beauty dismissing my suit
And she dropped me off in the city
With my books, and the Romans, and truth.

And, as she drove towards the horizon,
I knew I could never be free
For in dreams she'd return to haunt me,

A marriage that never could be.

Now all I have left is this vision,
A beauty dismissing my suit,
A loss I have chosen to live with,
With my books, and the Romans, and truth.

Aisling Gheal: (Irish) 'a bright vision'. During the eighteenth and nineteenth centuries some of our most powerful poems belong to the *aisling* type, political poems in which the poet encounters a vision-woman of great beauty, the spirit of Ireland, who foretells the coming of a Stuart redeemer.

To My D-28

Your body's unblemished
And sweetly you're strung,
A beauty I dreamed of
Since I was young,
But I'm middle-aged
Losing hair, overweight,
And it's now you come to me,
My D-28.

As youngsters we dreamed
And talked of guitars,
We played out our crushes
On prized Yamahas,
And though we made music
When out on a date,
We wished we were playing
A D-28.

We played Epiphones, Yamahas,
Fenders – all good;
We played on them music
To suit every mood,
But deep down we dreamed
That sooner or late
We'd all find our very own
D-28.

The past becomes present,
The dream becomes true.
It was music I loved, dear
(I thought it was you);
You're all that I dreamed of

But now it's too late
For I'm pledged to another,
My D-28.

And still we make music
But now we both know
That there's no going back
To the long, long ago
For my road is taken,
I'm resigned to my fate,
My first and forever
D-28.

The Ballad of Joe Fitzmaurice

The phone call came from Uncle Mick
To hurry to Tralee,
The hospital had phoned him
And he needed me.

The hospital had told him
That Joe was close to death
And I should go to be with him
His last few hours on earth.

In Annagh Ward on Level 2
The matron said to me
'Your uncle took a sudden turn,
He's very weak;

If anyone needs to see him
Go to the phone and call,
There might be no tomorrow
Though I don't have a crystal ball'.

And in I go to Uncle Joe,
Who thinks that I'm a nurse,
And I have seen my people die
But this time it's worse,

Joe writhing on the pillow
On the verge of sense,
Aware that he was dying,
Terrified and tense.

I prayed that he'd die easy
As I held his hand

And the chaplain came and prayed with him
And he seemed to understand.

'Hail Mary' – still he knows it,
He prays along with her
And when the prayer is over
He makes a little stir;

'It's all right, Joe', she soothes him,
'You're in Our Lady's care'
And she holds his hand and rubs
What's left of Uncle's hair.

'I want, I want, I want', he cries
Tugging at his clothes,
'Our Lady will look after you'
The chaplain calmly goes,
'I want, I want, I want', he cries –
'I want to blow my nose'.

The chaplain takes her leave of us
But Joe can find no sleep –
'Hail Mary', 'Holy Mary',
'Hail Mary' he repeats.

And this is all that's left him
On the edge of consciousness,
A prayer taught by his mother
To ease his last distress.

I join in the 'Hail Mary'
So he'll know he's not alone
Then hold his hand and rub his hair
And go out to the phone.

He Barks at His Own Echo

He barks at his own echo
All day and all night long;
He barks at his own echo,
He thinks he's not alone.

He barks at his own echo
And the echo answers back,
Whether he knows who's barking
It still is good to bark.

Whether he knows who's barking
It still is good to bark.

The *Díseart*

A sign points to the *Díseart*,
A place of prayer and art –
An empty convent chapel
Whose private Harry Clarkes

(Twelve stained-glass lancet windows)
Are public here today,
And some come here for beauty,
And some come here to pray.

Once I prayed in beauty
In the sanctuary of art –
How much was self-deception?
What now is Harry Clarke?

What signifies the light
That's filtered in this place?
In this convent chapel
For some it still means grace.

But I leave the chapel,
It's given me no peace
(I'm through with self-deception),
Face the teeming streets.

Nothing was transfigured
But I saw things in his light,
A beauty not sufficient
To transform my plight.

And yet, the heavens streaming
Through windows stained to art

Illuminate the darkness
In the chapel of my heart.

Díseart: (Irish) a retreat, a hermitage; a deserted place, a desert
Harry Clarke (1889–1931) was Ireland's outstanding stained-glass artist.

Heroes

Maybe there are no heroes –
Just people that we cheer
In our need for glory
Born of our fear

And the heroes we are cheering
Are much the same as we
As fear of being nothing
Is changed to poetry.

At the Car Wash

The things we take for granted!
Take the washing of a car –
Take Frank Burke this morning
In the family garage:

I asked him for a car wash
And he, in cleaning it,
Revealed himself in washing
As he scrubbed the mud and grit.

Most people when they wash a car
Take care with the parts you see –
They're the superficial ones.
But the ones who care beneath

Knowing 'twill soon return again
To its former state,
They're the undefeated,
The ones who, day by day,

Clean the underside of things,
The parts you never see,
The ones who take in breakdowns
And tend them constantly.

Moyvane

Am I reading you, my native place, all wrong?
In reading you, is it myself I read?
Is the village I have turned into song
Real only as a figment of my need?
The characters I see, to other eyes
Are bogmen at home only in a drain
(What do critics do but criticise?);
They survive their critics just the same.

Which is real? I ask myself again;
Is insight a reflection of oneself?
What I make eventually of Moyvane
Is what I make eventually of myself.
What I am depends on what I see
As vision proves itself in poetry.

I and the Village

A trap, a haycart and an empty street
(An image that I've carried all these years),
A greyhound at the corner where we'd meet –
A picture of the past, too deep for sneers.
Jimmy Nolan took that photo 'way back when
His camera was the only one around.
The village of my childhood. Once again
I'm a child, and this, my native ground,
Is empty as a Sunday afternoon
When pubs are closed and all are at the match;
I sit at Brosnan's Corner on my own,
Empty as the street where I keep watch –
An emptiness he pictured like a poem;
An inward street: the street that leads to home.

The Meades

Oh, that first night the Meades came to Moyvane!
A pub band with vocals, organ, drums,
The first such band that came here; they'd no van –
Just the leader's car with speaker, microphone,
Drums and organ loaded in the boot;
They'd come from the next village – up from Glin,
Dressed in Sunday best, no flashy suits,
A staid and sober band that drew us in.
Now Mikey Stack takes off his trusty cap
And sings for us (he's never sung before),
And husbands waltz with wives while single chaps
Tear in to comely maidens 'round the floor.
A sleeping village woke the night they came.
Nothing after would ever be the same.

Country Life

It's not so much that I'm out of fashion –
It's more that what I do was never 'in';
Oh sure, they paid lip-service, doled out rations
In some pie-eyed back-to-basics Gaelic dream.
And yes, we're still surviving, dancing, singing
At the crossroads where our betters turned away.
We choose to make a life here while they're clinging
To a past that we who live here know is fey.
And yes! they come on visits to the country
To see a past they say we should 'preserve'
As if we country folk were merely sentries:
When they come back, they get what they deserve –
A place that they no longer recognise,
A progress that they, tourists, must despise.

On Declining a Commission to Write 200-Word Biographies of Irish Writers for Their Portraits in a Hotel

They put the writers' portraits on the wall –
It fills a space and elevates the tone;
Later, they might hold a festival –
No matter that the writers wrote alone.
Everyone is at it, shops, hotels –
It brings in tourists seems to be the ploy;
Like wallpaper, it suits the decor well,
And when the tourists come, we know they'll buy
Aran sweaters, crystal, Celtic kitsch,
Harmless stuff that tourists take away
(Budget stuff, up-market for the rich)
To remind them of their Irish holiday.
They've the writers where they want them – on the wall,
Backdrop to the muzak in the mall.

Scorn Not the Ballad

Scorn not the ballad: it's the tale
Of lives like ours (and told without a fuss).
Sing it with a glass of flowing ale!
What's ours belongs to none, and all, of us.
No other verse can sing us like it does,
No other verse can wring out of the past
The strange, familiar melody that flows
Like truth from all who raise the singing glass.
Scorn not the ballad! Sing it out
In every public house, in every street;
It wasn't made for parlours – hear it shout!
Though sober as a sonnet, hear it beat.
You can't escape its rhythm, rough and rude;
You hum along not caring if you should.

I Don't Care if What You Sing Is Shite

I don't care if what you sing is shite,
There's more than words will make this world worthwhile;
What offends by day will sing at night
As day resolves itself. In a moment I'll
Be asked to sing a song and then I'll strive
To sing something that the drinkers all will know –
The kind of song that keeps this pub alive,
A poetry that never fails to show
A people who are sung, and thus exist
In a songline where a melody will bring
What words alone cannot to those who're pissed,
The kind of song we all half-know and sing.
You know us by the songs we sing at night,
The sentiments we keep by day from sight.

In the Dark

for John Mole

Evenings Jimmy Mac and his wife Jo
Would sit in their own kitchen after dark
In the silence of true peace. No radio
Disturbed them, and if outside a dog would bark,
The peace inside was multiplied. No light
Was turned on; they both would sit content
As darkness fell and twilight turned to night;
This was a house that knew what darkness meant.
If light draws moths to brilliance, then the dark
Drew ramblers to that kitchen, old and young;
Out of the glare, these night-souls would embark
To find within themselves the source of song,
That bypassed place that opens up at night
With fireside songs that don't survive the light.

The Heroes of My Childhood

The heroes of my childhood are unsound:
Age has brought amnesia, and the fact
Is lost, irretrievable in a mind
That makes a gallous fiction of the act.
The old men all are heroes in their own
Stories that they tell me of the past;
I listen, for respect must still be shown –
The men who built this state are dying fast.
Tradition tells us what we need to know,
The truth that can't be proved about ourselves;
I listen well, observe tradition grow
Vital and unsound as old men's tales –
Such stories as have made us what we are:
For this we live and die and go to war.

Gallous: a composite word incorporating 'gallant', 'callous' and 'gallows'.

Alzheimer's Disease

'They're hanging me this evening', Mary says,
Or else it's a transplant she must have,
But her concern's observing the Fast Days
(The cares of childhood follow to the grave);
'Am I going to Mass on Sundays?' she repeats
(How the good are frightened of their Church);
All we can do is comfort with deceit;
She's satisfied, and then begins to search
For biscuits, the indulgence of her life –
She'd eat them by the packet were she let,
A humble and obedient country wife;
Everything we tell her she'll forget,
But not the past – the past is as today
Where she was damned unless she would obey.

Lassie

At ninety years he fell into a drain –
That's what John Bradley tells me from his bed
(Hospital plays tricks on old men's brains);
But for his dog, he tells me, he'd be dead.
How fact and fiction make us what we are –
He fell at home at bedtime in the dark
(The drain was years ago outside a bar);
His faithful dog had more sense than to bark –
She lay down on her master all night long,
Licked his face and wrapped him from the cold,
And when the ambulance came to take out John,
Lassie stayed and couldn't be consoled.
She guards his house and lets no stranger through –
When there's nothing left, love finds such things to do.

To a Guitar

Frowned upon by purists: rightly so –
So many have done violence to the tune;
Playing you, I've learned all I know
Of music – how it can raise or ruin.
I've seen men take up the fiddle and destroy
Everything they have in music's thrall
For music's not a thing that we enjoy –
It's a gift that, once it's granted, takes all.
In giving all, we risk all that we are,
There's no hiding when you play a jig or reel
(Even if you're strumming a guitar) –
You're nothing there but what you think and feel.
And it's worth it to make music, take that chance.
You're, either way, a partner in the dance.

Knockanure Church

A place of worship, simple and austere;
'Sixties architecture past its date.
I wonder what it is that draws me here
To a building local people seem to hate.
The church of their affection, knocked, made way
For the 'garage on the hill' in its design –
Bare brick, flat roof, no steeple, here I pray.
The spirit of this building's kin to mine.

My God's a God who strips me in this place –
No cover here, the lines are stark and spare;
Through the years, I've grown into this space
Where work of human hands raised art to prayer,
The same the builders raised up once at Chartres
But plainer here, an answer to my heart.

The Mortuary Card

The snaps we use are chosen for their smiles,
No frown will mar the memory of the dead;
And so, the one that's chosen from the piles
Of old photos is chosen for the head
And shoulders. Cut out from the group
(A wedding, perhaps, carnation in lapel)
Without his cap, before old age and stoop,
We see the man we want to see. We tell
Ourselves that this is how he looked in life:
Usually he didn't, but so what?
Useless to plead with daughters, sons or wife
To show him as he was; for what is caught
In the photo on the card his loved ones show
Is the man that doesn't die, the soul they know.

In Memory of My Father

Since my father died, I've changed. It seems
That I become my father more and more;
I carry him around, awake, in dreams
Who followed me alive. Now his door
Is locked. House closed, I have my father's key;
I open the familiar, room by room –
Not just a house, it's more a memory.
The house itself must not become a tomb
So I open up the windows, light the fire,
Decide which clothes I'll give to charity
(The rest I'll burn later in a pyre),
Host a farewell for the family
Who share in this last supper, wine and bread,
Who resurrect the memory of the dead.

A Corner Boy

'Take therefore no thought for the morrow: for the morrow shall take thought for the things of itself. Sufficient unto the day is the evil thereof.'

The Sermon on the Mount

Just lazing at the cross with friends and neighbours,
Just gossiping the morning hours away,
Returning to the time when we, teenagers,
Learned to stand and wait, an idle day,
When dogs curled up and slept at Brosnan's Corner,
When our lives stretched out before us like a haze,
When everything seemed happier and warmer –
Ah yes! Those were the very best of days.
And here I am again at Brosnan's Corner
Gossiping the morning hours away.
No! The past was neither happier nor warmer –
Sufficient is its evil to the day.
I stand here with my back against the wall,
Take no thought for a world in its own thrall.

You Trust Me When I Leave You for the Wild

for Brenda

You trust me when I leave you for the wild –
The poetry, the pub, the after-hours,
The kind of trust that often is defiled
By love betrayed and guilt's false gift of flowers.
My life's a search for poetry; but you,
Content to know the word's not certain good,
Brenda, are everything I know that's true
While I, your poet, am volatile as mood.
I leave you for the wild, you go to sleep –
I come home late, my head pub-full of lore;
I go down to our room, pull up the sheet
And duvet round your shoulders; then sit more.
You trust me no matter where I go
With a trust (it's said) that only children know.

A Sonnet for My Wife

My love will take no bullshit. Not from me.
She knows me well, especially when I try
To tint with roses everything I see:
She knows it's self-deception; that I lie.
No! My love grows roses that are real –
The ones you plant and care for all your life,
Blossoms that we both can smell and feel,
Blossoms that I pluck for you, my wife.
And when the black spots come, the roses' blight,
Collapsing self-deception, your belief
Will not give up, as I, without a fight:
You tend the rose and bring it love's relief.
No! my love will take no bullshit for she knows
That tinted love will not support a rose.

Double Portrait au Verre De Vin

after Marc Chagall
for Brenda

She takes him on her shoulders; he is light
As the angel that descends about his head;
Mounted on her shoulders, all is bright
(Long enough he's lived among the dead).
He sits upon her shoulders; he is light
As the wine he raises in the glass is red;
Man and wife – no! lovers: in the night
He'll pour himself into her on their bed.
She takes him on her shoulders; dressed in white,
This is the dress she wore the day they wed;
She raises up her love to such a height
He sees the angels dance about his head.
She takes him on her shoulders; he is light.
Mounted on her shoulders, all is bright.

from The Boghole Boys

(2005)

The Playman

for Father Tom Hickey

You took Moyvane, a poor, passed-over place,
And showed the world a village in its grace;
You took Dev's comely lasses, sturdy lads
And walked us through the crossroads. I'm glad
I was alive in your time, growing up
In a village that played Beckett, where every pup
That hung about the Corner House had seen
The Nunans – Collette, Dympna, Gerardine –
Transform themselves, and us, upon the stage.
You rehearsed us in the spirit of the age.
Thanks to you, good Father, we learned to play
Our part in the drama of the day.
You understood your village and released
The poetry within us, playman, priest.

The Poet Strikes Back

He opes his lips! Let no dog bark!
Sir Oracle, Lit. Crit.,
Descends upon the work of art,
A fly upon a shit.

The shit is good and necessary,
It fertilises land;
What's a fly do? Spreads diseases.
I swat it from my hand.

The Celebrant's a Critic or He's Lost

The celebrant's a critic or he's lost
The soul of his own people in a blind
Elevation of his parish at the cost
Of putting the obnoxious from his mind.
They shit on us, these upstarts who return
To the pubs in which they drank; I know their breed –
They boast to old acquaintance as they burn
With all the ostentation of their greed.
Fuck off with your money as you stand
Buying off misfortune at the bar;
I'm a celebrant and though you shake my hand
And act as if in friendship, this is war.
I stand up for my people, mind them well,
I know your kind, your money. Go to hell.

Poet to Poet

I'm sending this though I don't think I should,
My sheaf of poems – took all my life to write.
I need to know if they're any good.

These little poems contain my sweat and blood;
For years I've kept them hidden out of sight.
I'm sending this though I don't think I should.

You won't offend me if you should conclude
That this old lady's poems don't make it quite.
I need to know if they're any good.

My husband laughs and tells me I delude
Myself, such stuff should never see the light.
I'm sending this though I don't think I should

But it's better to know the worst than brood
So I'm sending them (though in not a little fright).
I need to know if they're any good.

Forgive me if you think that I intrude
But a poet like you will surely see my plight.
I'm sending this though I don't think I should.
I need to know if I'm any good.

The Ballad of Rudi Doody

A song

My name is Rudi Doody
From Kildeboodybeg,
I'm one week out from Ireland,
Here in Winnipeg;
I'm off to make me fortune
In a land beyond the sea
But I'll ne'er forget where'er I roam
What me mother said to me.

'Goodbye Rudi Doody,
Off to Winnipeg;
Remember Moody Doody
In Kildeboodybeg;
Write a letter now and then
And send us the few pound –
The more we get, the more we want
Till we're six foot underground.'

Then one day a letter came
From far-off Winnipeg
Announcing Rudi Doody
To Kildeboodybeg;
He came all rings and biros,
And boasted in the pub
That he could buy the whole damn place
And give every man the sub.

He spent three weeks in Ireland,
Stood all his mates a round,
Staggered to the butcher shop
For the best of steak in town;
And then, the three weeks over,

He packed his case again,
And the cock crew in the mornin'
As he boarded on the plane.

Meanwhile back in Ireland
In Kildeboodybeg,
His mates all toast this *dacent* man
In far-off Winnipeg;
But as the years roll onward,
He comes back less and less
For the kids at home drink with their own –
They don't know who he is.

Goodbye Rudi Doody,
Off to Winnipeg;
Remember Moody Doody
In Kildeboodybeg;
Write a letter now and then
And send us the few pound –
The more we get, the more we want
Till we're six foot underground.

The more we get, the more we want
Till we're six foot underground.

Mairg Nach Fuil 'Na Dhubhthuata

after the Irish of Dáibhí Ó Bruadair (c. 1625–1698)

Oh to be pig-ignorant
With money in the bank
Among these boors and upstarts,
Their tabloid *Daily Wank*.

Oh to be pig-ignorant
Then I wouldn't see
'The Sunday Poem' passed over
For the strippers on page three.

A Local Murder

They all know the murderer
But there's a worse disgrace –
To be an informer
In your native place.

One summer's day a stranger,
Innocent of this code,
Stops for a drink of water
At a cottage on the road.

Suspicious of the stranger,
Yet country courtesy
Invites him to her kitchen;
They small-talk, he and she,

And, looking out the window,
He admires the view;
When it's time to take his leave of her,
He asks, as one will do,

What that nearby hill is called.
Standing at her door
'As true as God, good man', she says,
'I never saw it before.'

The Day Christ Came to Moyvane

He came to fix umbrellas,
Kettles, basins, pans;
The squad car turned in my yard
And jumped the tinker man –

'What are you doing?', 'What's your name?',
'Get going out of here';
The tinker man walked down the drive,
My dog snapped at his heels.

But the tinker man was used to dogs,
He just kept walking on,
And as he walked he whistled
And was gone.

The Guard was doing his duty –
There had been reports
Of travellers casing houses.
I'd been robbed before,

So I thanked the Guard and offered him
A beer, a cup of tea,
And as we talked, the tinker man
Walked farther away from me.

Before the Word 'Fuck' Came to Common Use

Before the word 'fuck' came to common use
(Even toddlers going to play-school know it now),
Before the lid was raised on child abuse,
We said that we were innocent. But how?
We heard the whispers and we went along,
Protecting those who were above the law
In a world we eulogise ('knew right from wrong'),
A world nostalgia paints without a flaw.
Before the word 'fuck' came to common use
We were children and our masters ran the show . . .
Guilty as condemned, it's no excuse
To plead that in the past we didn't know.
Before the word 'fuck' came to common use
Children mattered less than their abusers.

The Mission Magazines

They're in decline, the *Africa,*
Mission Outlook, The Far East,
The divine word is dying
With its nuns and priests.

This testament to piety,
These little acts of hope
With pictures of the mission lands,
Their saints, an ageing Pope

Are in decline like religion
In the disillusioned West,
They leave a void behind them
And our defining quest

For eternal truth and beauty
Is consumed like booze
In headlong self-destruction
We call our right to choose.

They're in decline, these pieties,
Relics of the past
In an age of self-expression
Where nothing's said to last.

On Hearing Johnny Cash's
American Recordings

The great ones have the courage to believe,
The courage to go naked if so called,
To pare life back to where things don't deceive;
Let those ashamed of feeling be appalled,
These simple songs of love and death ring true
In an age when we're afraid to show the heart –
'Whatever you say, say nothing', this in lieu
Of a creed that years ago joined prayer and art.
We say nothing and mean nothing now that we
Lose belief and, cynics in our loss,
Look down on the believer, this poetry –
The gospel of a soul that takes its cross,
Songs a life has earned or else are trash,
Salvation, suffered, sung by Johnny Cash.

Double Portrait with a Painting by Chagall

'Double Portrait with a Wine Glass'. Marc Chagall.
The coupling of true lovers in their bliss,
A song of songs of love before the Fall
More joyous than his portraits of a kiss.
The bird of love transports us here to see
This couple raise their wine-glass once again;
We celebrate our anniversary,
The covenant I made on wedding Brenda,
Lovers as Chagall and Bella here
Floating in their love above their town.
Come to me and mount my shoulders, dear,
Come to me, an angel for your crown,
I bare my breast, support you. Have no fear.
When the wine is drained I'll lightly set you down.

His Last Pint

He came into the village one last time,
Defying cancer by an act of will
As he came into the village in his prime.

He left with me as his clock began to chime
Nine o'clock; swallowing a pill,
He came into the village one last time.

We stopped at Kincaid's Bar; he couldn't climb
Out of my car until I helped him. Still,
As he came into the village in his prime,

He walked in unsupported, and I'm
Certain that the drinkers felt a chill
As he came into the village one last time.

He called for a Carlsberg and lime –
Too weak now for the Guinness that he'd swill
When he came into the village in his prime.

But the cancer couldn't take his state of mind:
From the tap of life the dying drank his fill –
He came into the village one last time
As he came into the village in his prime.

The Village Schoolmaster

1. Among Schoolchildren

These children here in front of me are . . . what?
Neighbours' sons and daughters sent to school,
Little friends who heed me, sometimes not,
Who, years hence, might join me on a stool
In the local pubs as I grow old:
One by one, they'll saunter to the bar;
Now and then the odd one will make bold
As young bucks flaunt their manhood, jar by jar.

These children here in front of me are good,
They're all that I could hope for in the young,
They'll serve their parish well in adulthood
(The kind of thing that often goes unsung),
And some will leave, and some, perhaps, will find
That greater place – the parish of the mind.

2. The Road to Damascus

She looks me squarely in the eye
And says (no trace of fright),
'You think you're the biggest man in the world',
And, to my shame, she's right.

I persecute with learning,
Make her, and others, fail
In the name of education.
It's I, not she, who've failed.

This, then, is the moment,

Struck from my high horse,
I see the child before me –
Child most wondrous.

She looks at me, offended,
Her accusation mild.
Who would become a teacher
Must first become a child.

3. The Lone Star Trail
for Gerard Quinn

It started as a song –
A simple round
Of cowboys and of cattle

Till sound possessed the children,
Who yelled
And neighed
And mooed:

Cowboy was a horse
And both were cattle.

Then the song became their pictures,
Swift and rude.

They offer me their pictures for approval
(All suns and no horizons) . . .

I approve.

4. The Hurt Bird

After playtime
Huddled in the classroom . . .

In the yard
Jackdaws peck the ice
While the class guesses
The black birds:

Blackbirds?
(Laughter).

Crows?
Well yes . . .
But jackdaws.
Those are jackdaws.
Why do they peck the ice?

Wonder
Becomes jackdaws' eyes
Rummaging the ice

Till suddenly
At the window opposite –

Oh the bird!
The poor bird!

At the shout
The jackdaws fright.

Sir, a robin sir . . .
He struck the window
And he fell
And now he's dying

With his legs up
On the ice:

The jackdaws
Will attack it sir,

They will rip its puddings out.

I take the wounded bird,
Deadweight
In my open palm –

No flutter
No escaping

And lay it on the floor near heat,
The deadweight
Of the wound
Upon my coat.

Grasping
The ways of pain,
The pain of birds
They cannot name,
The class are curious
But quiet:

They will not frighten
The struggle
Of death and living.

Please sir,
Will he die?

And I
Cannot reply.

Alone
With utter pain

Eyes closed

The little body
Puffed and gasping

Lopsided
Yet upright:

He's alive,
The children whisper,
Excited,
As if witnessing
His birth.

Would he drink water sir?
Would he eat bread?
Should we feed him?

Lopsided
The hurt bird
With one eye open
To the world
Shits;

He moves
And stumbles.

I move
To the hurt bird:

The beak opens –
For food

Or fight?

I touch
The puffed red breast
With trepid finger;

I spoon water
To the throat:

It splutters.

Children crumb their lunches,
Pleading to lay the broken bread
Within reach of the black head.

The bird,
Too hurt to feed,
Falls in the valley
Of the coat,
And as I help
It claws
And perches on my finger,
Bridging the great divide
Of man and bird.

He hops
From my finger
To the floor

And flutters
Under tables
Under chairs

Till exhausted
He tucks his head
Between wing and breast,

Private
Between coat and wall.

The class
Delights in silence
At the sleeping bird.

The bird sir . . .
What is it –
A robin? –
Look at the red breast.

But you never see a robin
With a black head.

I tell them
It's a bullfinch,
Explaining the colours why:

I answer their questions
From the library.

And the children draw the bullfinch –

With hurt
And gasp
And life

With the fearlessness of pain
Where the bird will fright

And in the children's pictures
Even black and grey
Are bright.

5. Getting to Know You

Thomas,
You don't trust me –
I can tell from your trapped eyes.
How can I help you,
My sulky friend?
Tell you I love you?
(That would seem like lies).
To reach out to touch you
Might offend.

Give you your head;
Watch over
In so far as any human can;
Coax you with tacit kindness;
Greet you, man to man . . .

Yes, Thomas,
I am strong
(But equal) –
And, Thomas,
We are both 'at school':
Both circling round
A common understanding,
Both sniffing at the smile
That sweetens rules.

Today you bounce up to me,
Your eyes the rising sun:

We share your secret story –

Hello!
God bless you,
Tom . . .

6. Primary Education

He put on the blues this morning,
Blue shirt, v-neck, blue tie –
The stamp of conformity.
His own clothes would defy

The system we impose on him –
He can't wear what he will:
How different is a uniform
To our desire to kill

The little spark of genius
That makes us different?
In my schooldays, I remember,
Everybody went

Dressed as they had clothes to wear –
Those of us with shoes
And underpants were 'sissies';
If we could, we'd choose

The bare feet, short pants, no 'knickers'
Of the jealous tots-to-twelves.
For freedom isn't granted.
We win it from ourselves.

7. The Interview

'How would you sell yourself as a teacher?'
What can I say but a teacher's not for sale,
That our choice of word often will betray us;
She's interested, but I can see I've failed

To convince her of the value of this reading,

That, a teacher, I'm bound to pass along
The values inherent in our language,
Values I'd inculcate in the young.

I could if I would blow my own trumpet,
Dazzle with achievement – then she'd see
What selling is, and all of pence and ha'pence,
But I'm suspicious she's not opened my CV.

This, then, is the system that I work for –
Blessed are the glib for they shall gain;
'What profit it a man to gain the world . . .'
I whisper to myself to keep me sane.

8. A Teacher Sings the Blues

I've never found the time
To indulge the child within –
All day I'm teaching children.
There are times I could give in

It's so lonely in the classroom,
And the kids don't understand
That I, too, hurt like they do;
And my! how kids can wound.

At lunchtime I'm 'on duty',
I patrol the shrill school yard,
A sandwich and a cuppa
In my hand. Oh, it's so hard

To keep an eye on children,
And if one of them gets hurt
You wonder if they'll sue you
And you've never been in court.

And the kids are getting bolder
And you know this could be good
Because, a child, you'd no such freedom,
You did as you were told.

And when you retire on pension
With forty years put in,
They'll make a presentation
In the local Arms or Inn;

And you'll look back, if you're lucky,
On a job, you hope, well done.
Then shortly you're forgotten –
You know that life moves on.

9. Death of a Teacher

The most public man in the village,
A teacher performs, is on view;
At fifty, he cannot continue.
Alas, what else can he do?

Fifteen more years to retirement
And half-pay the rest of his life,
His kids have ambitions for college
And he won't make a slave of his wife.

So he stands there alone in the classroom,
Too shrivelled and dry to shed tears,
Alone in a riot of children,
He clocks in the days and the years.

And the children grow up, leave the village,
The world is theirs while he stays,

Trapped in a vision that's crumbling,
He lives out the rest of his days.

Trapped in a vision that's crumbling,
He lives out the rest of his days.

10. On the Death of a Pupil

The requiem ends through children's happy cries –
It's playtime in the yard in his old school:
No one who's a child thinks they will die,
It takes a while to learn that life's this cruel.
The children playing football play their game,
More gape at the coffin from the wall;
In his thirties, the kids don't know his name,
But I remember him, remember all –
The years he spent before me, a young boy,
A young life cancelled pointlessly by chance.
You don't expect to see your pupils die.
No doubt someone's said we should give thanks
For the life he lived, the good that he achieved –
Cliches that we need, are half-believed.

11. The Teacher
for David Mason

I wish away my life until the pension,
Hoping that, just once, I will connect
With sympathy that is beyond attention;
Instead I keep good order, earn respect.
Once I had a vision for my village –
I'd bring to it a gift of poetry;
Tonight the talk's of quotas and of tillage
And how the barmaid gives out beer for free.

188

And yet, I've not lost hope in my own people –
My vision was at fault; these people need
To sing and dance, get drunk below the steeple
That accuses them of gossip and of greed.
I mind their children, give them right of way
Into a world I've seen and try to say.

12. Geography Lesson

'What are the four directions?'
They all know what I'm at;
Not Tom – he goes his own way
('Right, Left, First and Last').

And which is the right answer –
North, South, East and West?
Fine if that's where you want to go
But for Tom, his way is best.

Right and Left and First and Last –
That's the way he goes;
North and South and East and West
Are only for those

Who travel by the compass,
But a compass has no place
In Right and Left and First and Last,
In what he has to face.

Right and Left and First and Last,
He'll make his way along
With North and South and East and West
To where neither answer's wrong.

13. Clearing Out His Classroom, a Teacher Gives an Old Globe to a Child

The world has changed since first I got this globe,
The map has changed, the climate even more;
Man's walked on the moon, and now we probe
Further space and plumb the planet's core.
The atom split, we split now, lobe by lobe,
The human being, desperate to explore
Ourselves, our world. In more sober
Times we lived without such answers. Sure
Times have changed; the world that old globe shows
Is kaput as ancient Egypt, Greece or Rome;
Nonetheless, for all the new world knows,
It's still looking for the word that makes it home.
You take this battered globe as though 'twere new:
The world is in your hands, depends on you.

14. On Being Appointed Principal Teacher of Moyvane National School

For my people who walked barefoot miles to school,
For the children in the years of hand-down dress,
For the hurt who can't forget being branded 'fool',
For the ones who left this parish to success;
For the youths that died in foreign wars, who fought
When adopted lands conscripted them, and those
Who lived and died for Ireland, those who wrought
A nation from a peasant's ragged clothes;
For those who perished homeless, those who took
Their lives in desperation, and for all
Who were wronged or felt diminished by the book,
For those who heard and followed its great call;

For all my predecessors have set free
From the days of the hedge school down to me,
I accept this post.

Keeper of the Story

for Dick Spring

1. To Pádraig Pearse
for Declan Kiberd

I see you, Pearse, in Dublin with your sword –
Cuchulainn (hardly!), a poser with a dream.
In the new State, our teachers often bored
Us pink with 'Ireland – How She'd Seem
To Pádraig Pearse'. I didn't give a damn –
Those essays were for old men to offload
Their hang-ups at new freedom. Pearse the man
Was never taught us – teachers toed
The party line in everything they taught;
A poet like Pearse was dangerous, and so
They cast him as our conscience, and some bought
It. I didn't want to know.
They forged you in their image, and I sought
A way to write those essays and to grow.

2. Knocklong

Oh, take me through the byroads
To those places named in song:
Along the road less travelled
Is the station of Knocklong,
Where shots rang out for freedom
In nineteen and nineteen
With young Seán Hogan rescued
By Seán Treacy and Dan Breen.

As I drive to Tipperary
I recall the lore,
The War of Independence –

Here I park my car
On a road become a songline
And walk into the song
'The Rescue of Seán Hogan
At the Station of Knocklong'.

The station's now deserted,
Blocked up, overgrown,
But not the gallous story,
An empire overthrown;
But I am overtaken
By the traffic on the road,
Who hoot at this obstruction,
The progress I have slowed.

And so I take the burden
Of history and drive
Into Tipperary,
Where I see New Ireland thrive;
But I'm glad I took the byroad
That led me into song –
Many roads to Tipperary.
Only one Knocklong.

3. Dan Breen
for Fintan O'Toole

> 'there's a great gap between a gallous story and a
> dirty deed'
>
> *– The Playboy of the Western World*

My Fight for Irish Freedom by Dan Breen –
I read it like a Western; I'd pretend
To be a freedom-fighter at thirteen –
It made a change from 'Cowboys'; I'd spend

My spare time freeing Ireland in my head,
Reliving his adventures one by one –
The policemen that he shot at Solohead,
Romance about the days spent on the run.

A nation born of romance and of blood,
Once ruled by men who killed for their beliefs,
Now a nation grown to adulthood,
Losing faith in heroes, tribal chiefs.
Dan Breen is laid with the giants who held sway;
The gallous reads of dirty deeds today.

4. Two Brothers
Two brothers joined the Column
To fight for *Ireland Free*,
Then the Treaty divided them;
The story that united
Shattered with the dream:
A man without a story
Is a man who must redeem himself.
The community of purpose
Shattered like a glass,
Each seeing his own image
Singly, piece by piece
Where once all life was mirrored;
He would again be whole –
Fighting for their stories,
Comrades, brothers, soldiers
Join in Civil War
And so did these two brothers.
They never again shared
Sleep beneath the same roof,
A pint in any bar,
Dinner at one table.
And so, the fighting over,

They both moved to the Bronx,
Married, raised families –
Never once
Did they communicate.
I remember as a child
Their (separate) summer visits,
Two storied men who smiled at me
And played my childish games:
I remember with affection,
At times recite their names
When opposite *is* opposite.
Some things won't unite:
Wounds will knit, not stories,
Till the poetry is right.

5. A Windfall

The Castle – Anglo-Irish – where the Knights
Held out despite the English through the years;
They fought, and, when it made no sense to fight,
Turned Protestant like many of their peers.
The Civil War. In 'twenty-two, the Knight's
An enemy of the people (so they say).
Some hotheads want to burn him out; one night
He's raided by the local IRA.
The old Knight in his wheelchair holds his ground –
If they burn the Castle, they must burn him too;
They won't kill him; they put their petrol down
And head back to the local to review
The situation. They don't return. (They're jarred.)
The Knight retains their petrol for his yard.

6. The Mother

Forced to view his body –
Her guerrilla son

Shot dead in an ambush
By an occupier's gun;

Forced to view his body
In the workhouse, where,
Lest there should be reprisals,
She could show no mother's care;

Forced to view his body,
She denied she knew her son,
Then left him to an unmarked grave.
That's how the war was won.

7. What the Provo Said to Me
Easter 2003

It was a true republican
I met that Easter day,
One who knew his history
And was not afraid to say

That the time for war was over,
That the end had come,
That, short of hitting London
With a nuclear bomb,

The time for war was over
Except for a die-hard few,
But that loudest against the ceasefire
Were a cowardly crew

Who suddenly were brave men
When the war was won,
All huff and puff and posture,
Who never fired a gun,

All mouth against the ceasefire,
Hangers-on he'd dub
'Fuckers who did nothing,
Patriots of the pub,

'While others did the fighting
When fighting was required,
I tell them when I see them
They were always on ceasefire;

'I tell those cowardly fuckers
They were always on ceasefire'.

8. Up the Republic!

No one listened to us
When we sang contemporary
So we changed to rebel ballads
And shamrock *graw-machree*.

We sing for local drinkers
Who cheer and dance and shout
And call the English 'bastards'
When whiskey, lager, stout

Have made them bar-room patriots;
We sing for Yankees too
Who, thinking that it's Irish,
Ask for 'Toor-

a-loor-a-loor-al',
That Tin Pan Alley song:
We Blarney-and-Killarney
Till the whole place sways along.

We could be singing better

(The stuff we used to sing)
But shut-eyed introspection
Won't make the rafters ring.

So it's bawl those rebel ballads
And every kind of shite
As we die for Ireland
Twenty times a night.

It's bawl those rebel ballads
Each night from half-past ten,
The sound-check done till the clock strikes one,
We're die-for-Ireland men.

Up the Republic!

9. On Being Refused Publication in *The Spectator*

My poems don't cross the borders of his land:
The editor's enjoyed them, but he writes
That the readers of his mag won't understand
So he's keeping these 'fine poems' out of sight.
My poems address my nation is his plea –
'Do they reach across the borders and address
The English who don't know your history?'
(Whose conquest left my country in a mess).
'You obviously have', he tells me, 'the right stuff
So I hope you'll send us some more poems anon';
As if he's not already said enough,
He holds my poems to show them to his Mum
Who's Irish, wed a Welshman – to my dismay –
'But they split up', he quips, 'so it's OK.'

10. Galvin and Vicars
In memoriam *Mick Galvin, killed in action, Kilmorna, Knockanure (in the parish of Newtown Sandes, now Moyvane) on Thursday, 7 April 1921; Sir Arthur Vicars, shot at Kilmorna House, his residence, on Thursday, 14 April 1921*

Mick Galvin, republican,
Arthur Vicars, who knows what? –
Some sort of loyalist –
In Ireland's name were shot:

Vicars by republicans,
Galvin by the Tans,
Both part of my history –
The parish of Newtown Sandes

Named to flatter landlords
(But 'Moyvane' today,
Though some still call it 'Newtown' –
Some things don't go away

Easily). Galvin and Vicars,
I imagine you as one –
Obverse and reverse,
Sundered by the gun.

History demands
We admit each other's wrongs:
Galvin and Vicars,
Joined only in this song,

Nonetheless I join you
In the freedom of this state
For art discovers symmetries
Where politics must wait.

11. On the Execution by the Irish Free State of Four Republican Soldiers at Drumboe, County Donegal, 14 March 1923

The Letter
of Lieutenant Timothy O'Sullivan to his mother
on the eve of his execution

Drumboe Castle,
Stranorlar,
Donegal.
13.3.1923.

Dear mother,

At 4 o'clock this evening
It was announced that I
With three others of my comrades
Tomorrow morning die.

It wasn't unexpected,
Let God's will be done;
I wouldn't change places
Now with anyone.

In Donegal they've offered Masses
To prepare us for this day,
We made a general Confession
To Father McMullen of Ballybofey;

The priest took our addresses
And will write to you,
We'll have Mass tomorrow morning,
Holy Communion too.

Dear mother, don't be troubled,
Let no trace of sadness lurk,
For I'm sure that God will judge us
According to our works.

I'll wear your beads tomorrow,
They'll be sent you with my clothes.
Goodbye again, God bless you
And my dear friends in Listowel.

My comrades send best wishes,
We all are treated well.
I forgive our executioners.
Mother dear, farewell.

Your fond son,
Timmy

12. The Guardian of the Dead

Keeper of the story
And guardian of the dead
(Soldiers of the Republic
'Executed'

By the Black and Tans –
'Murdered' is what he'd say),
He tends the roadside monuments
Of the fallen IRA

(The men of the Flying Columns
Of 1921,
Locals who, but for history,
Would have taken up no gun),

A man who's out of fashion,
A man who'll not be led;
Alone at the roadside monuments
He minds his dead.

Pádraig Pearse: Patrick Pearse, poet and teacher, an executed leader of the 1916 Easter Rising, which led to the foundation of the Irish Republic.
Column: i.e. *Flying Column*, an active-service unit of the IRA during the War of Independence.
Tans: i.e. *Black and Tans*, a unit of the Crown forces during the Irish War of Independence.

That's football!

for Mick O'Connell

1. At the Ball Game
for Seamus Heaney

Everything out there you see
Is a version of reality
As heroes triumph over doubt
And bring their kind of truth about.

Each, according to his way,
Engages on the field of play,
And, urging on, the faithful crowd
Are cheering, praising, cursing loud
For beauty only will suffice,
Beauty to infuse our lives:
No cup, no trophy will redeem
Victory by ignoble means.

And, so, we take the field today
To find ourselves in how we play,
Out there on the field to be
Ourselves, a team, where all can see;
For nothing is but is revealed
And tested on the football field.

2. Munster Football Final 1924

Nothing polarises like a war,
And, of all wars, a civil war is worst;
It takes a century to heal the scars
And even then some names remain accursed.
The tragedies of Kerry, open wounds –

John Joe Sheehy on the run in 'twenty four,
The Munster Final in the Gaelic Grounds:
There's something more important here than war.
John Joe Sheehy, centre forward, republican,
Con Brosnan, Free State captain, centre-field;
For what they love, they both put down the gun –
On Con's safe conduct, Sheehy takes the field.
In an hour the Kerry team will win.
Sheehy will vanish, on Brosnan's bond, again.

3. The Team of 'Sixty-Two
for Garry McMahon

No logo here on jersey, togs or boot,
A team who played for pure love of a game
That reveals its players in their truth,
A team that asked no money, handled fame.
We got a lift to the wonder of TV,
To a distant village, a small set in the hall,
We paid like all the others just to see
Our team's ascent to glory raise us all.
For we believed in heroes 'way back then
Who raised themselves to immortality;
Before me in that photo, fifteen men
Who from my youth were more than men to me.
That picture hangs where once a saint or pope
Would look down from the wall in pious hope.

4. A Footballer

He could have played with better
But he chose his own;
Playing with his county
He'd never carry home

The trophy all aspire to
But that's not why he played:
If he played with another county
He'd feel he had betrayed

Himself, his art, his people,
So he plays out his career
Away from the glare of headlines.
And yet sometimes you'll hear

From followers of football
The mention of his name.
It's enough that they believe in him,
His way, his truth, his game.

5. The Game of Your Life
for Bernard O'Donoghue

Whatever way it's kicked out, face the ball!
While wingers await delivery in space,
Centre-field must rise above the maul
And safely field, taking thought to place
The ball of fortune with the chosen one
And will him on to make the greatest use
Of what he's given: the ball passed on,
He solos towards the goal as play ensues.
For now's the time when great men must redeem
The story of the game from death, defeat:
The game of life's the story of a team
Who cannot rest until their task's complete –
To take the cup, the cup that cannot pass,
And raise it up in glory for the mass.

6. Dancing Through
Homage to Mikey Sheehy, footballer

Nureyev with a football,
You solo to the goal,
Where the swell of expectation
Spurts in vain –
O master of the ritual,
O flesh of tribal soul,
Let beauty be at last
Released from pain . . .

Now grace eludes its marker,
Creating its own space,
While grim defenders
Flounder in its wake;
And the ball you won from conflict
Yields to your embrace –
Goal beckons like a promise . . .
And you take.

For Eamon Lloyd

When Munster played the Tigers, Welford Road
Was the land of heart's desire for every fan;
Match tickets were more valuable than gold.
I travelled ticketless with my teenage son
Just to be there in Leicester on the day
With Munster men and women for the game –
To find a likely pub and watch the play
Was as much as we could hope for until Eamon
Lloyd, with whom we stayed, a Tigers fan,
Gave my son his season ticket for the match,
What money couldn't buy, this kindest man
Gave John his heart's desire. Old friend, we watched
The game on television. And Munster won.
'Twas nothing to your kindness to my son.

Mick Galwey

Local Hero, International Star

He was a county minor,
Played midfield but was slow,
Won an All-Ireland medal
But was smart enough to know

He'd not make it playing Gaelic,
So he switched to rugby and
Became an international hero
Playing for Ireland.

Playing Gaelic football's
Not too lucrative,
The rugby network
Had more to give,
Now instead of commercial travelling,
He's an executive.

At the famous playwright's funeral
The papers all were there
Noting the famous faces;
They noted this great player,

And in the queue I overheard
An old GAA man say
'If he was a small bit faster,
He'd be a poor man today'.

Poem for Nessa, Five Years Old

She brings me a pale strawberry
While I'm sitting on the loo,
The last one in the garden,
Says, 'Dad, this is for you'.

I don't know what I'd do without her –
There simply is no place
That she won't come and find me,
A smile upon her face.

For Nessa always finds things –
No matter what is lost,
Nessa's sure to find it.
She's found me in the past

When I've been lost and lonely,
Nowhere to lay my head,
She's brought me hope – like strawberries.
Who cares if they're not red!

Poem for John

A bucket on his head, a pretend soldier
Wearing Mammy's boots that reached above his knee . . .
He remembers this quite clearly now he's older –
The magic world he lived in, turning three.
He'd go to bed sitting on my shoulder,
His Daddy Doodle, oh so proud of me!
It's not that what's between us has grown colder –
To grow apart is part of being free.

I love you, son, as on the day you came
Into my life, a baby who would need
All I could give, my love, a home, a name,
My word made flesh though not born of my seed.
Tonight you put your teddy from your bed –
The magic wanes, the world looms ahead.

Table Quiz

The questions come out neatly one by one.
Son, each one has an answer that's precise;
No room for thinking here as, like a gun,
The mind fires out the answers. Here a voice
Whispers loud its knowledge like a boast,
All that can be known for certain's here:
There are winners, there are losers as we toast
A world where each question's answered clear,
A world where simplicity prevails.
Outside this circle nothing's answered thus,
This futile show of certainty that fails
Every decent question asked of us.
So spit out all the answers while you can,
Before the questions come that make a man.

Sick Child

He's too young to suffer, Lord, like this;
Take this burden from him, make it mine:
I've long put up with troubles; the abyss
I've long looked into. In denying
Whatever it is that troubles him, he pales
And pukes with what the secret won't admit;
Everything the doctors give him fails –
Is there nothing those doctors have can hit
The cause of his strange sickness and can cure
Whatever it is that troubles him this while?
I'd prefer to suffer than endure
Helpless while he suffers. He's my child.
Take this burden from him, hear my plea.
Let me take his load that it unburden me.

A Widower

They thought to make you marry when she died;
Accounts of matches came from women who
Would share your life should you take one as bride,
But, constant as your love for her was true,
You lived alone for nearly thirty years
In the home you made with Mam, an invalid.
I remember once you told me over beers
The reason why you did the things you did.
You said you'd bring no other to your life,
Fearing I, your only child, would be upset.
Not so, Dad: caring for your wife
You knew the love that lovers don't forget.
The others who would wed you came too late.
A love like yours would take no other mate.

Granada

My mother should have been here, but ill health
Confined her to her bed much of her life –
That, and her lack of worldly wealth,
Her meagre store, a village grocer's wife.
She'd read about it when she'd sight to read,
Heard it sung (in English) on LP;
Confined to bed, her mind was all she'd need –
To see it in the flesh she left to me.
Enough for her that she had heard its song;
Enough for her that, though she'd never see
Granada and all for which she longed,
Enough it was to know their poetry.
Through narrow streets, among the souvenirs,
I think of her through mingled sweat and tears.

Nerja

There are fewer to send postcards to at home,
My people have all but disappeared,
No one to call up on the phone,
No one to worry about over here.
I sit in my apartment looking out
On *Mare Nostrum*, but that sea's not mine,
This beaker full of the warm south,
The sun, flamenco and the Spanish wine.
Parents play with children in the pool,
The sun blasts down on pale skins oiled to tan,
Here on the balcony it's cool
As the hottest it ever gets to in Moyvane.
And there's no one I need call now on the phone:
The dead have taken with them much of home.

Home

My family are dying one by one,
My uncles and my aunts – just Peg now left:
The ones who, returning to Moyvane,
Brought England with them in the way they dressed.
They'd travel home from Shannon on the bus
(We'd no cars back then to make the trip),
Though a lifetime 'over', they spoke the same as us,
Still the same old Kerry accent rough and rich.
They never lost their Kerry: they'd no need
To lose themselves in England, or to pine
For Ireland lost as they passed on their seed;
My cousins are English, and our line
Still comes home to visit: they belong,
A people and a place that still are one.

The Fitzes Come to Town

Those sultry summer nights in Dinny Mack's,
The Fitzes home from England; the whole clan
Singing, dancing, drinking for the crack.
Those nights were the talk of half Moyvane.
Musicians came and played till closing time,
The Fitzes danced their old-time sets again,
Drink flowed like talk that's loosed by beer and wine,
And teens accepted shandies from the men.
Those sultry summer nights in Dinny Mack's,
All were welcome among the Fitzes, who
Brought the summer with them and relaxed,
Who never shirked when there was work to do.
And Dinny Mack would stand us the odd round,
Saying ''Tis better than the carnival when the Fitzes come to town'.

Cutting Grass in Glenalappa

In the name of all who went before us, we cut this grass:

The ones who farmed the homestead,
The rest who emigrated
To become firemen, policemen and domestics in New York,

Factory workers and navvies in London, Leicester, Sheffield,
Saint Helen's,
Thelwall, Dagenham, Watford.
In your name we cut this grass.

Know today you're not forgotten
As my son and I cut the grass you cut before us
At home in Glenalappa.

In the name of your sons and daughters, we cut this grass,
And their children
And their children's children;

And for the time when there's no Fitzmaurice left in
   Glenalappa,
When the family have scattered like seeds on the wind,
When all that's left here of the Fitzmaurices is green grass,

In the name of all those generations, today we cut this grass.

For the Fitzmaurices of Glenalappa

Nesta,
'Brood mare of the Geraldines',
Is where we began:

For six hundred years
Fitzmaurices, Fitzgeralds –
Nesta's clan,
Builders of abbeys
And castles,
Connoisseurs of poetry,
Horses and fine wine,
Were conquerors of the land.

But the Fitzmaurices,
Normans,
Had become 'more Irish than the Irish'
As time went on.

Our castles fell to Elizabeth,
The Lords of Kerry fell
(Except those who submitted
To England's will –
They kept their lands).

The builders of abbeys and castles
Are found in Kerry still
In small holdings
In glens like Glenalappa,
My ancestral home.
I travelled there this Christmas
With my son.

*

My father,
His father
And his father's father
Sat around the fire
At Christmas
In Glenalappa.

As I did.

The fire is out
This Christmas,
The house deserted,
No Fitzmaurice now
In Glenalappa.

Farewell
All the Toms, Dicks, Jacks,
Noras, Ellens, Margarets
In every generation
Who sat around the fire
In Glenalappa.

Where are you, this Christmas,
My people?

Everywhere but in Glenalappa.

And somewhere in New York,
First cousins I've never met,
Whose names I don't even know.

For all the fires that burned
At Christmas in Glenalappa,
For all the generations
Who sat around that fire,
For all my people,

Dead, alive or yet to be born,
For whom this place is home,
Out of our history
I make this poem.

Fitzmaurice of Glenalappa.

from Twenty One Sonnets
(2007)

On First Meeting the
Marquess of Lansdowne

Listowel Castle, 21 April 2005

The Marquess of Lansdowne is the direct descendant of Patrick Fitzmaurice, son of Thomas Fitzmaurice, 18th Lord Kerry. Patrick was five years old when Listowel Castle, the last Fitzmaurice castle to hold out against Queen Elizabeth I, was besieged by Sir Charles Wilmot in November and December 1600. He was smuggled out of the castle upon its surrender. Patrick, 19th Lord Kerry, was subsequently captured, educated in England and raised in the Protestant faith.

'Which line do you belong to?' I don't know.
Too poor to trace, there's no record of my line.
Somewhere, somehow, long ago,
Someone, a Fitzmaurice, one of mine,
Left it all behind him, and now I
Can't trace my line to castles. All I know
Is we left all that behind us, I don't know why,
But know myself a poet, proudly low.
A rich man with a title finds his place
In history. It was ever so.
The rest of us are hard pressed to trace
Our great-grandparents. It's enough to know
That, rooted in this place where I belong,
I turn our common history to song.

True Love

They didn't sleep together in the end:
'True love', Mam called it from their double bed;
Her illness made her husband her best friend.
He took no other mate when she was dead.
They didn't sleep together in the end:
From mid-life on, my father slept alone;
I wonder how he felt being her best friend,
But he didn't complain, and stayed with her at home.
They didn't sleep together in the end:
There's more to love than self – they both knew this;
They loved enough to call each other 'friend' –
That's what it meant each night when they would kiss,
Before Dad left their room to sleep alone.
True love it was. That's what kept them going.

Homage to Thomas MacGreevy

MacGreevy, poet, Catholic, you found your place
In a world where art redeemed, the word was true,
In a creed that raised living into grace
As, a poet and a Catholic, I must too.
The life a Catholic has to face
Is no different to the life we all go through,
Losing heart at the squalid commonplace
But for a vision that redeems its ugly hue.
So welcome, then, the hopeless and the base,
The depths descended as their artists drew
Their Christs amid dejection and disgrace,
Christ my muse in poem, in pub, in pew.
With MacGreevy, poet, Catholic, I find my place
In a creed that raises living into grace.

A Middle-aged Orpheus Looks Back at His Life

for Kris and Lisa Kristofferson

I took my voice to places where no man
Should take his voice and hope that it would sing.
All I wanted when I began
Was to strike up my guitar and do my thing.
Haunted from home, I sang my song
While all around forgot their words and fell;
In the underworld I blundered on
In regions where not it, but I, was hell.

I took my voice to places where no man
Should take his voice and hope that it would sing;
I paid the price in lines that rhyme and scan,
The last illusion to which singers cling
Before they yield their song up to the truth
They thought they could out-sing in foolish youth.

from Poems Of Faith and Doubt
(2011)

Ruckard Drury

Ruckard Drury, *spailpín*,
Laboured all his life
For pig-ignorant farmers.
One day, a farmer's wife

Had Drury at her table.
Her fare was tea and bread
But she served him up bad butter,
Which Ruckard Drury fed

To a farm-cat at the table,
And when the wife saw that,
She turned on the *spailpín*,
Who replied: 'Do you see that cat?

'You gave me rotten butter;
You saw what he did, no doubt –
That cat there had to lick his arse
To take the taste from his mouth.

'That cat there had to lick his arse,
The butter was so bad.'
Then Drury left her table
And the daily bread it had.

Drury left her table
Hungry still, but proud;
A *spailpín*, he's remembered
Hungry but unbowed.

Ruckard Drury.

Ruckard Drury: Ruckard (Michael) Drury was born in the Bog Lane,
Knockanure, in the parish of Moyvane in 1864 and died in 1952.
Spailpín: (Irish) a migratory farm labourer.

My Father Hired with Farmers at Fourteen

My father hired with farmers at fourteen –
No time for school, there were siblings to be fed;
He worked, a servant boy who farmers deemed
Barely worth their shillings and a bed.
My father hired with farmers at fourteen;
He took the boat for England when he could,
A servant boy no more, he'd not be seen
The victim of some farmer's whims and moods.
My father hired with farmers at fourteen
While I, precocious, a selfish little brat,
Strutted out book learning. I was mean:
I'd never know the places Dad was at.
My father hired with farmers at fourteen;
He made damn sure his son was free to dream.
Thanks Dad.

The Fiddle Master: Homage to Pádraig O'Keeffe

for Eugene O'Connell

School's no place for artists who can't take
The ravages of teaching: it destroys
The soul, once full of singing, that must break
As the vision that sustained it shatters, dies.
Not so O'Keeffe, the fiddler: to survive,
He packed the whole thing in one fateful day.
The inspectors on his case, he couldn't thrive
In the classroom. So he left. O'Keeffe would play.
He played throughout Sliabh Luachra, where he taught
Music to his people, who revere
A musician and a teacher who only sought,
In return for his fiddling, his fill of beer.
It killed him in the end, this way of life,
The man who took a fiddle for his wife.

To My Son as He Leaves Home

Son, just to have you 'round the house is good,
The way you make your presence felt. I'll miss
The way that being with you was drink and food;
The future beckons, now it's come to this.
You're leaving, son, I wish you all the best,
May every good that life can give be yours,
Stand firm, love, when life becomes a test,
Remember that the good you do endures.
You're leaving, son, take all you need from me,
It's freely given as it was when you
Needed me, a baby on my knee,
Needed me as to a man you grew.
I love you son, I shed a happy tear
As I let you go in faith and hope and fear.

To My Daughter, Pregnant

She brings me eggs from chickens she has reared,
Cabbages and carrots she has grown,
All the things about her for which I feared
Have come to naught: she's come into her own.
She brings me eggs from chickens she has reared,
Soon she'll be a mother. I rejoice.
Daughter, from the moment you appeared,
You gave me songs to sing in joyful voice.
Soon you'll be a mother and you'll give
Not eggs just but a grandchild to adore,
Another reason for a man to live,
For a grandchild adds its blessings to our store.
Pregnant with the life in which you bloom,
You bless us with the child within your womb.

Death of a Playwright

In memoriam *John B. Keane*

'John B. is dead', Listowel said,
Incomprehension on its brow;
'John B. is dead', Listowel said,
'We're only an ordinary town now.'

The Last Wren Boy

In memoriam *Eddie Cunningham*

They brought their celebration
To the darkest time of year,
Lighting up midwinter
With music, song and beer.

Before Saturn was forgotten,
The wren boys played their part;
Now the state we live in
Has breathalysed the heart.

Farewell to winter revelry,
The sacrament of night,
We have no need of wren boys
In artificial light.

We have no need of wren boys,
We have no need to give
Libation to the darkness
That the light might live.

Farewell to you, last wren boy,
You blessed my home today,
You played and drank my whiskey
And went upon your way.

Farewell to you, last wren boy,
High priest of the dark,
You brought your light here with you,
Behind you, left this spark.

You brought your light here with you
And left it in my heart.

'Help Me Make It Through
the Night'

The old lady greets Kristofferson with
'You must listen to my story,
How you helped me make it through the night.

'I was a married woman with four children
And my Church decreed it wasn't right
To use contraceptives with my husband,
So I'd scrub the floors at bedtime
Till my husband was asleep
And the only company I had,
The only help in my plight,
Was you singing over and over
"Help Me Make It Through the Night".

'And how once I was in Saint Patrick's Purgatory,
A penitential island where I went
To walk barefoot, hungry, thirsty,
That I might learn what my life meant
And in confession to the priest there
I opened, heart and soul,
And told him that we had four children,
That at nights I scrubbed the floors
Because the Church didn't allow contraceptives,
That, on my knees till my husband slept,
That only then would I cease scrubbing
And retire to our marriage bed.
I asked him to advise me
But he left me dead –
He couldn't help me and my husband
Was all he said.

'So know when you sing that song again, Kris,
That I see it in this light –
A woman on her knees scrubbing.

'You helped me make it through the night.'

'Would You Believe'

for Mark Patrick Hederman

Would You Believe on TV Sunday night,
'The Church in Crisis' the subject of debate;
I watch it in the pub, my Church's plight,
'The Pope's a Nazi' one drinker snorts in hate.
Everyone here is Catholic; some object
That they come to the pub for company and chat,
Or else a show with which they can connect;
They don't approve what this poor pilgrim's at.
I go to the loo, the channel's changed
To football – religion's turned them off,
(The new religion's sport, I don't complain
As I struggle with my Church, let who will scoff),
Catholics ignoring this debate:
The future of their Church. Too late. Too late.

A Community Mourns the Death, by a Freak Accident, of an Eighteen-Year-Old Boy

We've nothing to fall back on now but prayer
To a God who's either absent or is dead,
To commend our troubles to His care,
Not knowing if He's hearing what is said.
We've nothing to fall back on now but prayer,
To open to the power, the help of words
That they, perhaps, might heal us in despair
As we look into the face of the absurd.
We've nothing to fall back on now but prayer,
The common bond between us in our grief,
The trouble that we shoulder, that we share,
Crying from the trials of belief.
We've nothing to fall back on now but prayer,
The only hope that's left us in despair.

When I Pray

I talk to myself,
The only person
I can't lie to.

Whether God is listening
Or not,
I don't know
But I talk
As if He were.

I talk;
He doesn't answer.
Not that I expect Him to.

But wisdom comes
Through talking
As if God were listening,
Where only truth will do.

When I Die

Don't eulogise me with pious lies.

Tell them
I was a man of pubs,
A man of song,
But there were times
When even singing and drinking
Let me down;

Tell them
That I didn't believe enough
In myself or God,
That I didn't always live
As a good man should;

Tell them that I loved
But not enough,
Tell them that loving me
Was often rough;

Tell them I was selfish,
I was vain
But didn't diminish responsibility
Through pain;

Tell them I was no stranger to the dark
But was lit by stars
When the black dogs barked;

Tell them I was honest,
That I lied,
But remember to tell them also

That I tried.

Don't bury me with platitudes
About Christian death.

Say me like I was
And commit me to the earth.

from A Middle-aged Orpheus
Looks Back at His Life

(2013)

An Irishman Salutes the Queen

You came, you saw, you conquered, English rose,
No Caesar come to keep our people down,
You bowed to the memory of those
Who rose against your country and your crown;
The past at last forgiven, now it's time
To face the future confident that we
Can rise from hurt as, friends, in hope we climb
To live as equals, from ancient hatreds free.
For no more can hate or ignorance divide
(Oh! the bigotry in which we once were drilled),
I remember all the Irish who have died,
I bow before the English we have killed.
You came to us, a monarch dressed in green,
You understand your symbols. Welcome, Queen!

On Becoming a Grandfather

for Katie

I thought I loved until you came along,
No other love can now become a threat,
Love is faithful or everything goes wrong,
There's nothing I have loved that I regret.
I thought I loved until you came along,
You freed me up to be myself, and now
That I've found my voice again in song,
I sing with all that heaven will allow.
I thought I loved until you came along,
The ghosts that haunted me I now call friend,
I love all that I hid for far too long,
When I think of you, Kate, all my old hurts mend.
Never have I known a peace so strong;
I thought I loved until you came along.

My Girlfriends Now Are Other's Children's Mamas

My girlfriends now are other's children's mamas,
They've married well or broken up in pain,
The love we shared no one can now take from us,
For that alone I'd do it all again.
My girlfriends now are other's children's mamas,
Love let us down, oh! what a price we paid,
And yet we're friends (we never were piranhas),
Of all those loves my wife's the one who stayed.
My girlfriends now are other's children's mamas,
I think of them sometimes with deep regret,
We're older now, sensible as pyjamas,
We still are friends though we're apart, and yet
I pray for them and hope that life will bless
Those early loves that ended in a mess.

Just To Be Beside You Is Enough

Just to be beside you is enough,
Just to make your breakfast tea and toast,
To help you with the ware, that kind of stuff,
Just to get the papers and your post;
To hold you in my arms in calm embrace,
Just to sit beside you at the fire,
Just to trace my fingers on your face
Is more to me than all of youth's desire;
Just to lie beside you in the night,
To hear you breathe in peace before I sleep,
To wake beside you in the morning light
In the love we sowed together that we reap.
Together we have taken smooth and rough.
Just to be beside you is enough.

A Catholic Speaks Out

I'm through with cover-ups, I'm through with Rome,
To think that I believed them all these years,
From now on I'll worship God at home
And bid an end to all my childish fears,
Fears I learned in school where we were crammed
With all the shit the men in black prescribed,
Anyone who questioned them was damned,
They raised their poisoned cup and we imbibed.
I'm through with cover-ups, I'm through with Rome,
The thought-police can't reach me now I'm free,
And though I love the art of spire and dome,
The ritual and all it means to me,
I'm through with cover-ups, I'm through with Rome,
From now on I'll worship God at home.

In Extremis

They come to Mass, these kids who never come,
For their friend who took his life eight years ago,
Tonight's the night he'd have been twenty-one,
And still they feel the awful, shocking blow.
Tonight's the night he'd have been twenty-one,
A party night, instead they go to Mass,
Later of course they'll drink and smoke, have fun –
Anything they can to make time pass.
Later these kids will drink and smoke, have fun,
But first they go to Mass, that's what you do
When everything about you's on the run,
Even though your Church is damaged too.
Being here's the scraping of the pot
But, God Almighty man, it's all they've got.

New Poems

An Ageing Artist Looks at a Young Woman

When I was young and I saw beauty,
I wanted it for myself;
Now I'm older, when I see beauty,
I love it for itself.

For I no longer need to possess it,
It's enough for me
To be happy in your beauty,
Where it's enough to see.

I'm happy in your beauty,
Where it's enough to see.

An Ageing Artist Meets an Old Love

Once we were intimate,
Now we are polite,
Here a lifetime later
You're still lovely in my sight.

I could say I love you
After all these years,
The good times I remember,
I've repressed the tears.

And dammit! Yes, I love you,
I dream about you still,
There's much about this heart of mine
That's not controlled by will.

Yes, dammit! Still I love you –
Words I cannot say,
As we meet a moment
And go our separate ways.

On Hearing
'Sail Along Silvery Moon'

'Sail Along Silvery Moon',
The sound of summer when
We fell in love with teenage queens
Before we grew to men;

'Sail Along Silvery Moon',
You broke my heart and I
Descended to the underworld
To sing myself or die;

'Sail Along Silvery Moon',
The sound of summer when
We fell in love with teenage queens
And now I hear again

'Sail Along Silvery Moon'
But, alas, I am too old
To follow you across the sky –
My heart's grown cold;

'Sail Along Silvery Moon'
Rolling back the years,
Melting my heart of ice,
Turning it to tears;

'Sail Along Silvery Moon',
The sound of summer when
We fell in love with teenage queens.
I'm back in love again!

'Sail Along Silvery Moon'.

'Thank You for the Days'

Thanks for the years you gave me,
For keeping me alive,
For loving me in troubled times
When all I had to give

Was selfishness and music
As I toted my guitar
With every wounded troubadour
From bar to lounge to bar.

Thanks for the years you gave me,
I cannot give them back
But if I could, be sure I would,
And give you light for black.

Thanks for the years you gave me;
Every single day
I bless our times together
As I make my way,

Still singing, on that lonesome road
That leads to God-knows-where,
Around my heart a band of thorns,
The life that I must bear.

Around my heart a band of thorns
That I must turn to prayer.

La Belle Dame Sans Merci

He drinks all night in Kincaid's Bar,
His eyes as white as fear,
And never talks and never smiles –
He's doomed to live that year.

He met her first in Kincaid's Bar
And loved her for a price:
Now all he's left is Kincaid's Bar
And porter, cold as ice,

For porter's black – oh! as desire
And porter has its price
And once you whet, you can't forget
A thirst that's cold as ice.

She takes him to her grotty bed,
A year has him in thrall,
Then plies her charms in other arms.
Alone, with alcohol,

As morning dawns, the village yawns,
He searches for a pliers,
He takes the plug, the electric plug,
And strips the electric wires;

He wraps the wires around his wrists
(Oh Death, do not refuse)
And plugs into the socket
But only blows the fuse.

Denied by death, unloved by life,
His eyes as white as fear,

He never talks and never smiles,
He's doomed to live that year,

For love is black – oh! as desire
And love must have its price
And once you whet, you can't forget
A love that's cold as ice.

The Ballad of Timmy Mallon

Timmy was slow at school,
Couldn't count from one to two
(When it came to mathematics,
He hadn't got a clue);

And so one day the master
Took him by the hand
And explained mathematics
In a way he'd understand –

'Look here, Tim', the master said,
'I'll show you how to count,
Pretend that you have money
And tell me the amount

'In your trousers pockets –
In one pocket you've a pound
And in the other pocket
There's another pound;

'A pound, Tim, in each pocket –
Can you tell me what
Amount is in your pockets?
How much money have you got?'

Timmy lived in poverty
And so he scratched his head
And answered frankly: 'Please sir,
'Twould be someone else's pants', he said.

The Ballad of Tommy and the Sow

for Nancy McAuliffe

Everybody knew him,
'Tom, the village fool',
Who long ago, when just a kid,
Was the butt of jokes at school;

And all his life they laughed at him
For his simple ways,
How he barely could express himself,
His mind was such a maze.

One Sunday night he rambled
To a neighbour's house
Where the village gathered;
Tom sat there, anonymous,

Hidden in a corner,
While the others held court
Until one young smart alec
Decided, just for sport,

To play a trick on Tommy –
The sow had farrowed, and
He sent Tom to count the *bonhams*,
(The fingers of his hands

Were as much as Tom could calculate),
The litter was thirteen,
All knew that he could count to ten
And nothing more. He beamed

At those who laughed at him
As he set out to go

To count the *bonhams* in the shed,
But Tom was not as slow

As the village deemed him –
When asked for the amount
He proudly said, 'There's ten of them,
And the three I couldn't count.'

Oh yes! They deemed him village fool
(That's what they're remembered for)
But, remembered for his answer,
He's avenged in local lore,

He is. He's avenged in local lore.

Bonhams: piglets

Obsession

He had a strange obsession –
With catapult in hand
He went 'round breaking windows
In the village by the strand,
Ballybunion.

The police there gave him warning
They could tolerate no more,
Yet he went on breaking windows
In the village by the shore.

So they took him to Killarney
From the village by the sea,
Where they filled him up with tablets
And a course of ECT.

That fixed him – or it should have –
But when the doctors asked
Him what he'd do when he got home,
He'd answer with a laugh:
'I'll get a catapult
And I'll break every window in Ballybunion.'

So they keep him in Killarney
And every month or so
When they want to release him,
They can't let him go

Because he always answers
With the same old mad refrain,
Every time they'd let him out
His answer is the same:

'I'll get a catapult
And I'll break every window in Ballybunion'.

The months go by, he's still inside,
The long-stays ask him then
Why every time he's for release
He's kept inside again.

So he tells them of his answer,
The truth of what he'll do
Once he's home in Ballybunion.
The long-stays tell him: 'You,

'The next time you're asked that question
Tell 'em that you'll get
The paper for the horses
And you'll put down the odd bet;

'And tell 'em you'll go dancing –
Then they'll let you out,
But if they mention catapults,
Shut your mouth.'

Time goes by, he's called again,
He's ready this time and
He tells them what he'll do at home
In the village by the strand:

'I'll buy the morning paper
And I'll study the horses then
And I'll put down a bet or two';
The shrinks cry out 'Good man!'

'And I'll go to the dance', he tells them,
'And I'll go dancing with a girl
And I'll take her out and court her',

His head is in a whirl;

'Good man! Good man!' they urge him on;
'I'll take her out', he says,
'And I'll kiss her and then I'll put
My hand inside her dress';

'Good man! Good man!', they urge him on,
'And then what will you do?',
'I'll take the knickers off her',
'And then what will you do?'

'I'll take the knickers off her',
He continues with a shout,
'I'll take the knickers off her
And I'll rip the elastic out,

'I'll take the knickers off her
And I'll do what I've always done,
I'll make a catapult of the elastic
And I'll break every fucking window in Ballybunion.'

Biographical Note

Gabriel Fitzmaurice was born, in 1952, in the village of Moyvane, County Kerry, where he still lives. For over thirty years he taught in the local primary school, from which he retired as principal in 2007. He is author of more than fifty books, including collections of poetry in English and Irish as well as several collections of verse for children. He has translated extensively from the Irish and has edited a number of anthologies of poetry in English and Irish. He has published two volumes of essays and collections of songs and ballads. Poems of his have been set to music and recorded by Brian Kennedy and by RTÉ Cór an nÓg with the RTÉ National Symphony Orchestra. He frequently broadcasts on radio and television on education and the arts.

He has been described as 'the best contemporary, traditional, popular poet in English' in *Booklist* (US), 'a wonderful poet' in the *Guardian*, 'one of Ireland's leading poets' in *Books Ireland*, 'Ireland's favourite poet for children' in *Best Books!* and 'the Irish A. A. Milne' by Declan Kiberd in the *Sunday Tribune*.

Books by Gabriel Fitzmaurice

Poetry in English

Rainsong (Beaver Row Press, Dublin, 1984)

Road to the Horizon (Beaver Row Press, 1987)

Dancing Through (Beaver Row Press, 1990)

The Father's Part (Story Line Press, Oregon, 1992)

The Space Between: New and Selected Poems 1984–1992 (Cló Iar-Chonnachta, Conamara, 1993)

The Village Sings (Story Line Press; Cló Iar-Chonnachta; Peterloo Poets, Cornwall, 1996)

A Wrenboy's Carnival: Poems 1980–2000 (Wolfhound Press, Dublin, Peterloo Poets, 2000)

I and the Village (Marino Books, Dublin, 2002)

The Boghole Boys (Marino Books, Cork, 2005)

Twenty-one Sonnets (Salmon Poetry, Cliffs of Moher, 2007)

The Essential Gabriel Fitzmaurice (Mercier Press, Cork, 2008)

In Praise of Football (Mercier Press, 2009)

Poems of Faith and Doubt (Salmon Poetry, 2011)

A Middle-aged Orpheus Looks Back at His Life (Liberties Press, Dublin 2013)

Poetry in Irish

Nocht (Coiscéim, Dublin, 1989)

Ag Síobshiúl Chun An Rince (Coiscéim, 1995)

Giolla na nAmhrán: Dánta 1988–1998 (Coiscéim, 1998)

Children's Poetry in English

The Moving Stair (The Kerryman, Tralee, 1989)
The Moving Stair (enlarged edition – Poolbeg Press, Dublin, 1993)
But Dad! (Poolbeg Press, 1995)
Puppy and the Sausage (Poolbeg Press, 1998)
Dear Grandad (Poolbeg Press, 2001)
A Giant Never Dies (Poolbeg Press, 2002)
The Oopsy Kid (Poolbeg Press, 2003)
Don't Squash Fluffy (Poolbeg Press, 2004)
I'm Proud to Be Me (Mercier Press, 2005)
Really Rotten Rhymes (Mercier Press, 2007)
GF Woz Ere (Mercier Press, 2009)
Splat (Mercier Press, 2012)

Children's Poetry in Irish

Nach Iontach Mar Atá (Cló Iar-Chonnachta, 1994)

Children's Poetry in English and Irish

Do Teachers Go to the Toilet?/An dTéann Múinteoirí go Tigh an Asail?
  (Mercier Press, 2010)

Essays

Kerry on my Mind (Salmon Publishing, Cliffs of Moher, 1999)
Beat the Goatskin Till the Goat Cries (Mercier Press, 2006)

Translation

The Purge (A translation of *An Phurgóid* by Mícheál Ó hAirtnéide)
  (Beaver Row Press, 1989)
Poems I Wish I'd Written: Translations from the Irish (Cló Iar-
  Chonnachta, 1996)

The Rhino's Specs/Spéaclaí an tSrónbheannaigh: Selected Children's Poems of Gabriel Rosenstock (Mercier Press, 2002)

Poems from the Irish: Collected Translations (Marino Books, 2004)

Ventry Calling (Mercier Press, 2005)

House, Don't Fall on Me (Mercier Press, 2007)

Lucinda Sly: A Woman Hanged (Liberties Press, 2013)

Editor

The Flowering Tree/An Crann Faoi Bhláth (contemporary poetry in Irish with verse translations) with Declan Kiberd (Wolfhound Press, 1991)

Between the Hills and Sea: Songs and Ballads of Kerry (Oidhreacht, Ballyheigue, 1991)

Con Greaney: Traditional Singer (Oidhreacht, 1991)

Homecoming/An Bealach 'na Bhaile: Selected Poems of Cathal Ó Searcaigh (Cló Iar-Chonnachta, 1993)

Irish Poetry Now: Other Voices (Wolfhound Press, 1993)

Kerry Through Its Writers (New Island Books, Dublin, 1993)

The Listowel Literary Phenomenon: North Kerry Writers – A Critical Introduction (Cló Iar-Chonnachta, 1994)

Rusty Nails and Astronauts: A Wolfhound Poetry Anthology (Wolfhound Press, 1999) with Robert Dunbar

'The Boro' and 'The Cross': The Parish of Moyvane-Knockanure (The Moyvane-Knockanure Millennium Book Committee, 2000) with Áine Cronin and John Looney

The Kerry Anthology (Marino Books, 2000)

'Come All Good Men and True': Essays from the John B. Keane Symposium (Mercier Press, 2004)

The World of Bryan MacMahon (Mercier Press, 2005)